POLO VISION

The author photographed at the Whitfield Court International Polo School

POLO VISION

Learn to play polo with Hugh Dawnay

Hugh Dawnay

J. A. ALLEN
London

First edition published 1984

Reprinted 1986

Second edition 1991

British Library Cataloguing in Publication Data

Dawnay, Hugh
    Polo vision: learn to play polo with Hugh
Dawnay. 2nd rev. ed
    1. Polo
    I. Title
    796.353

ISBN 0–85131–539–9

Published in Great Britain by
J. A. Allen & Company Limited,
1, Lower Grosvenor Place,
Buckingham Palace Road,
London, SW1W 0EL

Book production Bill Ireson

Printed and bound by the Bath Press, Avon

I would like to dedicate this book to three people.

First my late Father, David Dawnay, who gave me a wonderful equestrian background through providing me with so many good horses and polo ponies to ride.

Second Colonel Alistair Tuck who restarted post-war polo in my regiment, the 10th Royal Hussars, by using great initiative to purchase and transport twelve Arab stallions from Baghdad to Aqaba, Jordan. There he organised and taught polo on the beach.

Third Brigadier Heski Baig who once generously coached a team that I was in and gave me many of the ideas that I have written here.

CONTENTS

Contents

The illustrations are by Susanna Holt and the photographs by MacInnes Photographs Limited, Dublin.

NOTE TO THE SECOND EDITION

Since writing the first edition of *Polo Vision* I have, for eight years, had the opportunity to watch most of the world's best polo players at Palm Beach, while I was there to conduct my Polo Vision Clinics. As new points, whether big or small, occurred to me I was able to experiment immediately with the people under my instruction.

Every year I have watched some of the Argentine Open polo matches and in 1988 had the privilege of working with Gonzalo Pieres (10) and Tollo Fernandes O'Campo (6) when we instructed a clinic together at their joint facilities near Buenos Aires.

I have also, in conjunction with Snoopy Productions, produced the first *Polo Vision* instructional video tape. This covers half of my book, using many good examples from the Argentine Open. The experience of making this video together with the many hours editing film of these superb players has given me further depth of knowledge and new ideas.

THE IMPORTANCE OF THE COACH

I continue to be amazed that so few polo players are coached and that the majority of polo teams put extra pressure on their best player by relying on him to do all the coordination without help from a sideline coach. To say that you never cease to learn is an understatement. Good coaches and players learn something from every match. My biggest problem is to keep remembering all the new points and to be able to recall them at the appropriate moment during a polo clinic. Nevertheless I am confident that my original 21 chapters are still the basis for my instruction today even though I have since introduced many valuable new points and minor changes. These are now explained in the extra chapters (Chapters 22 onwards) which besides providing more depth for my *Polo Vision* instruction, demonstrate the many different ways that exist for a coach to help.

FOREWORD

by Julian Hipwood, *Captain of the England polo team*

In *Polo Vision*, Hugh Dawnay has written a book which should fill a long empty place on the bookshelf of every polo player.

I found the book enormously interesting, not only for the beginner, for whom it is primarily intended, but also for all low-goal players, irrespective of their years of experience; it will also be useful for any player of up to five goals — one can never stop learning, and we all have faults or develop bad habits which need correcting from time to time.

Every aspect of the game has been covered: horsemanship, tactics, striking of the ball, and many of those little secrets of the game which only come through years of experience. Undoubtedly the author has profited greatly from his years of Army polo, and through the trials and tribulations of instructing the many pupils passing through his polo school in Ireland. The resulting book presents a formula for the learning of polo which is considerably easier than the game previously appeared to the uninitiated.

A very positive foundation in polo will be found by anyone reading this informative book.

Julian Hipwood
England, 1984

AN AMERICAN APPRECIATION

by Tommy Wayman, *Captain of the United States polo team*

I watched Hugh Dawnay's Polo School at Palm Beach Polo and Country Club in Wellington, Florida, and was impressed by the rapid progress of both beginners and intermediate players.

Polo Vision is an account of the same progressive approach. I believe it will quickly instil a sound understanding of the game and eliminate some of the bad habits which beginner polo players normally acquire. It will show them the quickest route to become an effective player in a game of polo and I therefore recommend everybody to read it.

Tommy Wayman
United States of America, 1984

Chapter 1

INTRODUCTION

The poet Firdausi described a game of polo played in 600 B.C. between the Persians and the Turkomans. In Iran today the remains of two stone goal posts, eight yards apart on a ground three hundred yards long, can be seen at Ispahan. These are the dimensions for a polo ground today. Hence the game can claim to be the first team sport ever to have been played.

What is meant by "team sport"? There is a very special and profound meaning. Yet many people, who join a team, play more as individuals than in the interest of the team. Ideally they should place the team first and their own desires second. This may involve a sacrifice in order to play a part which is vital to the team.

In polo more than in any other sport good team play is the best way to win a match. Although all four players need to reach a standard of considerable skill before they can combine effectively together, actually partaking in good team tactics is the quickest way to improve.

Modern polo had its early origins in India. Records show that in 1859, at Cachar, the Silchar Polo Club was founded by British cavalry officers and tea planters. Previous to this they had been introduced to the game by the Manipuris who lived in the northern mountains of India and had already played polo amongst themselves for at least two hundred years. It is thought that the Manipuris alone had kept the game alive because the many wars of those two centuries had never penetrated the remote valleys where they lived. From Cachar the game spread rapidly to other parts of India including Calcutta where a club was formed in 1862.

Polo in India was in due course written about and described in the *Field* magazine. Officers of the 10th Royal Hussars (the regiment I was to join many years later) were so enthused by such articles that they experimented by hitting a ball with walking sticks while riding their chargers. Later, they went to Ireland to buy suitable ponies. In 1870 the 10th Royal Hussars challenged and defeated the 9th Lancers in the first ever public polo match in Europe. A hundred years later the 9th Lancers took their revenge in a match of eight-a-side played at Windsor to commemorate the occasion. I was on the losing team but am proud to say that the event is recorded in the renowned book, *Chukka*, published in 1971 by Herbert Spencer.

In 1873 the Hurlingham Club of London took up polo as an extra sport. In 1874 their committee drew up some rules for the game to be played with five players in each side. Soon afterwards teams were reduced to four because it was found that such was the speed of play it was unsafe for more than eight participants to be on the ground.

The game spread rapidly in Britain and it was the British who were to introduce it to many countries in the western world. Initially the velocity of the game was checked by an offside rule and by a height limit of 14.2 hands for polo ponies. Both were abolished but not before various tricks had been employed to make ponies appear smaller than they were.

The British and Indian cavalry regiments stationed in India became highly proficient at polo and attained a very high standard, which was maintained until the beginning of the Second World War in 1939. How did this happen? In each regiment there was the equivalent of a small polo school where all newcomers could be taught most of the skills by one or more of their brother officers. Besides this all officers participated in equitation and horse mastership as part of their job. An inter-regimental tournament was staged annually and was given great prestige. Added to all this there was the opportunity to play high-goal polo with the Maharajas and all the best Indian polo players. Many of those Indians, such as the famous Hanut Singh, were prepared to discuss and teach ways of improving team and individual skills.

Some regimental teams became so good that their joint handicaps were higher than what would be accepted in British high-goal tournaments today.

For example, the 10th Royal Hussars had a team of twenty-five goals with which they won the inter-regimental of India in 1936 and the equivalent tournament in England in 1937. My father, who had a handicap of seven, played for them in both these tournaments and, in between, captained the 1936 British Olympic Team in Berlin, using the same ponies for the three different occasions. This was to be the last Olympics which included polo. The British team reached the final where they were comprehensively defeated by Argentina.

The United States of America has had many wonderful teams. These were highlighted when playing for the Westchester Cup. On thirteen occasions between 1886 and 1939 Great Britain and the United States battled for this famous cup. Except for one break in tradition, in 1936, the previous winner was always host for the next series. Britain won the first three times after which the United States was the victor nine times out of ten. This international competition engendered much interest in the sport of polo and greatly influenced some changes in the conduct of the game. For example, after losing the cup in 1909 the British realised that the offside rule was suppressing their standard of play and duly abolished it to conform to that of their opponents. Defeat in 1914 by a lighter British team on fast ponies, caused the Americans to examine ways of offsetting their disadvantage of having bigger and heavier players. Hence, they raised the height limit on ponies during the First World War after which Britain and all other countries followed their lead.

Throughout all the Westchester Cup encounters the standard of play and sportsmanship was outstanding and this good example did much to cause a boom in American polo in the era before the Second World War. Yet, in the Cup of Americas series, played between the United States and Argentina on six occasions since 1930, the United States only won the first. Some of the recent matches between them, played in Texas during 1980, were close enough, but the Argentine top player never brings his best pony out of his own country. He needs them for the next Argentine open and always plays abroad on his second string of ponies.

Argentina was one of many countries to which Britain exported polo. The Argentine horse is made for the game, although, strangely enough, the horse was not indigenous to the country. It is descended from the horses brought to South America by the Conquistadores. However, much Argentine farmland is perfect for breeding and training horses. A strong grass is grown and on it horses can fully develop without requiring any other feed or nutrition. There are thousands of large flat *estancias* on which the horse is widely used for controlling stock. Polo fields, in any number, can be marked out. Initially the farmers used the same ponies for rounding up cattle and playing polo. As the standard improved more and more players commenced selective breeding and the two types of pony began to look rather different. The cattle pony was, and is, known as a *criollo*. The British in South America at the end of the nineteenth-century crossed the *criollo* with the English thoroughbred to make the ideal polo pony.

As a result of these developments the numbers of players grew rapidly and the standard improved enormously. Even children were playing in their early 'teens. Some of them started hitting a ball from a tiny pony, often bareback, when they were as young as seven years old. Many clubs were founded all over the country including the capital, Buenos Aires. The Argentine is so vast, with its varying climate and geography, that it is possible for the enthusiast to travel and play polo all the year round within the borders of this one country.

Nearly all the owners of the *estancias* have houses and offices in Buenos Aires. As a result it was, and still is, relatively easy for the best players to congregate for a series of tournaments in this one area. The Argentine spring,

September to November, is the ideal time and over the years three big open tournaments have evolved. Two clubs, Los Indios and Tortugas, combined to organise one tournament, Hurlingham is the scene for the second and the one and only Argentine Open takes place at Palermo.

Whoever wins at Palermo can rightly claim to be the best polo team in the world. The Coronel Suarez team was handicapped at forty goals for half a decade up until 1979. Not only was each player playing off a handicap of ten, but they were all worth their handicap in the position in which they played. Yet, on many occasions, other Argentine teams have made Coronel Suarez battle until the last minute or even into extra time before accepting defeat. On one or two rare occasions they have been actually defeated. In 1975 Argentina had eight players with a handicap of ten goals, four with nine and five with eight goals. All played inside Argentina with 100% amateur status.

My lucky year was 1970, when I made my first visit to this Mecca of polo. I was playing for the British Army in a series of games against Argentine military teams. We lost every match but at a lunch before the final game I met Maria Ines, my wonderful wife. Since that first visit I have returned several times to Argentina and have seen many of the big matches. Clearly the Argentines are so far ahead of the rest of the world that it would appear impossible for any other country ever to compete against them successfully.

Yet obviously it is the desire of many players and the Polo Associations of their countries to attempt to close this gap. Hence the question must be asked: "Why is it that there is virtually no organised system of instruction and coaching in these other countries?" Not only should all beginners have the opportunity to catch up on what his Argentine counterpart has learnt on the *estancia* as a child, but at every handicap there

could be coaching for individuals and teams in a search for general improvement. Bjorn Borg and Sebastian Coe, two of the most outstanding athletes of all times in tennis and athletics respectively, have had, and still continue to have, coaching! In all types of football it is considered impossible to win unless a team has an outstanding coach who instructs and draws the best skills from individuals and then moulds them into one successful team. The managers and coaches of some of the best soccer clubs in the world were not themselves top players. Yet the outstanding players of today, valued at a million pounds, gladly heed the ideas and instructions of many such men. In the polo world there must be the same type of man whose talent is being wasted while many a high handicap player fails to achieve the best rating in his reach, some medium-goal players with great potential never break into high-goal and hundreds of low-goal players continue to chase the ball into obscurity.

At the time of writing it has been seven years since I opened the Whitfield Court International Polo School. In that time it has been my privilege to teach people from twenty-five different countries. The ages of my clients have varied from thirteen to sixty-two years old and fifteen of these were women. The majority were beginners but some had already played polo for as long as twenty years. I cannot imagine anything more rewarding than helping a person who is completely lost on the polo ground, begin to find a way of taking part in the proceedings. Obviously there are many different methods of presenting and teaching polo. I hope that the following chapters, which make-up the subject matter of a four-and-a-half-day course at Whitfield Court will be helpful to a few more beginners and show a new point of view to some of the established players. The experiences and stories that could be told about the happenings at the Whitfield Polo School during these seven years would by themselves fill another book.

Chapter 2

PLAY FOR FUN

Polo is a sport which gives all the players, win or lose, a chance to have fun. The pleasure of combining with others while enjoying the thrilling sensation of riding on horseback at speed and hitting a ball, must be second to none in all sport.

However, to maximise this pleasure, a player should know what he is doing. To achieve this he will need to learn tactics, polo riding and the technique of striking a ball.

There are various ways a player can acquire this knowledge and thereby improve his game and have more fun into the bargain. Coaching is one way and I believe it to be the best method for all standards of polo player, as it can be graded to the individual's abilities and talents and at the same time instil the basic skills which is, of course, essential in a team sport.

METHOD

My own methods, which I practice at the Whitfield Court International Polo School in Ireland, are designed to improve the player but not bore him in the process. I base my instruction on fifteen points, these being explanatory sub-divisions of the three basics — tactics, polo riding, striking the ball.

I have tried in this book to mirror this approach. Learning any new skill or sport is stimulating but it can sometimes be wearying where details and routines must be absorbed until they are second nature. To avoid too much repetition, I have not tried to teach all in one go all there is to know about one position or shot or tactic. I have presented information in the order in which I present my polo courses at Whitfield, that is with a logical sequence, frequent change of subject, practical work and the use of exercises.

For example, experience has proved that it is beneficial for students to have the roles of No.1 and No.4 — the two easiest positions at either end of a team line-up — clarified and exercises and shots carried out as relevant to them, before moving on to the other positions.

I have described the way a group can practice and achieve the necessary riding skills in order to gain the maximum from the exercises and then how to put them into operation on the field of play.

We have seen that to play polo is to have fun, and to play it very well will give us immense pleasure. However, even the best players are still learning and it will help all those involved in polo, of any standard, if they will keep in mind the three basic sub-divisions.

These might well be posed as three questions:-

Where to go? — tactics.
How to get there? — riding.
What to do on arrival? — striking.

Each time we learn more we get closer to answering these questions and gain more knowledge which, hopefully, we will put into operation next time we play a game.

I suggest there are three "do not's", one attached to each of the three questions posed above. These "do not's" will help us in answering the questions. They are:-

Don't chase the ball;
Don't look at your pony;
Don't hit too hard.

There are fifteen points which grow out of these questions. My method is to teach these points which, if studied and practiced along with the exercises, should lead on to a greatly improved personal performance in a player and a successful reputation for a team.

Where to go
Is a tactical problem. We shall discuss this in five sub-divisions: all-round vision; always adjusting; four positions; early closing; early turning.

How to get there
Is a matter of being able to ride correctly. We shall need to learn: outside your pony;

weight on saddle front; look and go; minimum use of hands; strong legs.

What to do

Is the technique of striking the ball. We will learn: place pony to ball; stick and hand position; use of shoulders; sweet spot; follow through.

TACTICS

All-round vision

Means that a player is constantly looking all around him to see everything that is happening, and being aware of the actions of the other seven players on the ground. Even when pursuing the polo ball you should know what is taking place behind you. As you battle in a ride-off you should be aware of all other players on the ground. Some players are ball-chasers, others ball-watchers. This prevents them from having all-round vision and consequently interferes with anticipation and correct positioning.

Always adjusting

Can only be achieved through all-round vision. Four players on a polo ground three hundred yards long are operating on the equivalent of three soccer pitches. You could say that they are doing the work of thirty-three soccer players. Therefore, the amount of adjustment required is immense and continuous. A player should never be satisfied with his position even when the rest of his team are between himself and the ball. A slight or large adjustment to the play is always necessary.

Four positions

Must be continually filled by the team of four players. If one player is out of position the team is down to three players and the loss in territorial control is enormous. You can be out of position by being too close to, even alongside, another team member. Being too far away, such as a No.1 being too far up the ground or a No.4 being too far back, is just as bad.

Hence, all-round vision is principally used to observe a player's own team, enabling him to adjust into the vacant position left by the other three. Normally the position is his own, which quickly becomes vacant if sufficient adjustment is not made. On some occasions another position is vacant, whatever the reason, and must be filled. There are rules for each position and these must be obeyed by all players as they fill their own or another position.

Early closing

Is the way to gain possession of the ball, once a player is in position. There are two types. One is closing to ride off an opponent. The second is closing to join the line of the ball. This is the line along which the ball is running or, in the case of a stationary ball, the line along which it was moving before it stopped. If the opponent is already on the line, then the two types coincide. A ride-off between two opponents is normally won by the one who starts to close first, the earlier the better. Through winning the ride-off the ball can be won. Otherwise the man who first closes to and joins the line can win the ball. It is the equivalent of two cars on a side road, with the same destination. The one which reaches the main road first should arrive at their destination earlier than the other.

Early turning

Is the way to win possession of the ball after the play has changed direction. In fact the player should turn before the play does. The player who turns earliest will win. However it is essential that he has adjusted into the correct position before turning. Thereby he will be able to join the line of the ball early and close first onto any opponent who threatens.

A player who has all round vision and is always adjusting into his correct position, will be able to close and turn earlier than his opponents.

RIDING

Outside your pony

Means that a person rides throughout a

White correctly spread out in four positions. Black badly positioned in a bunch, and too close

game without looking at the pony. Besides giving a player all round vision this will give him far more control and increase the manoeuvreability of the pony. It could be described as separating the heads of the pony and player. Nearly all horsemen continuously look at their horse's head to see what will happen next. It is better if the reverse happens so that the horse knows what to do next. All high-handicap polo players are outside their ponies, possibly without realising it. I have found that nearly all beginners and low-goal polo players coming under my instruction were inside their ponies.

Weight on saddle front

Is important for two reasons. Firstly, it is more comfortable for the pony and, secondly, it will position the player's body so that he can hit the ball correctly. With the feet fully home in the stirrups, the body weight can pivot at the thighs instead of on the balls of the feet. The latter makes a player stand in the stirrups to hit a ball and it has been taught for a long time in Europe and the United States. The former is the style used by the majority of Argentinians whose prowess in polo speaks for itself. Pivoting their body weight on the thighs instead of the stirrups has three big advantages: (1) You are closer to the ground; (2) You are more secure as you turn your shoulders; (3) You are independent of the pony's stride. This will be referred to hereafter as the "fork position".

Look and go

Is an extension of being outside the pony. A player should look sideways or backwards to see if a turn is required. If it is, he should then turn his pony keeping his eyes fixed in the new direction that he is going without looking down or at his pony. While looking sideways or backwards the player's weight should lean acutely towards the new destination. On being asked to turn, the pony will immediately want to be once more under the weight of the player. Hence the turn will be the quickest possible and the player will never lose sight of the relevant part of the game.

Correctly on the fork, outside pony

Minimum use of hands

    Is very important for a smooth performance by player and pony. The majority of control and steering should be done by the indirect rein so that any direct pulls on the pony's mouth are minimised. The bit in a pony's mouth is similar to the brake in a car. If it is over used there will be a progressive wear which will end in destruction. During the initial damage there is no evidence of wear taking place and hence no warning of the problem to come. For a car new brakes can be fitted but, for a pony, another mouth cannot be obtained.

Strong legs

Is a principle which is fundamental to all types of riding. The squeeze of the legs, correctly executed, tells a horse to stop, go slow, or speed up. In polo there is a continual change of pace and direction requiring many instructions from the players' legs. The best way to strengthen the legs is to ride without stirrups, initially for a few minutes progressing to at least fifteen minutes a day.

STRIKING

Place pony to ball

Is important because, for every shot, there is a specific position for the ball in relation to the pony. Even a shot hit through a difficult angle can be made easy if the correct position of the ball is used. A player should start placing his pony as early as possible. A bad ball-chaser rushes to the ball and tries to place his pony only during the last stride.

Stick and hand position

Is the actual place from which each shot should start. For the ten shots which will be taught in later chapters there are five different positions. These are advocated to introduce the correct swing and to make the player economic. The good, experienced player can be extravagant like a rich man, whereas the rest need the economy of a poor man. Otherwise the ball will constantly be hit late or missed.

Use of shoulders

Is vital in polo as in many other sports such as tennis and boxing. During every shot there is a moment when the shoulders of the player should have turned from being at right angles to the pony to a position parallel with the pony. If this is achieved it will obviate the use of arm strength by the player and assist him to hit accurately.

Sweet spot

Is that part of the polo ball which should be struck by the centre of the head of the polo stick. Instead of looking at the whole ball a player should focus on the relevant spot. For example, before shooting at goal, if a line is drawn from the centre of the goal to the ball the sweet spot is where the line would emerge after passing through the ball. To see this spot clearly the player must put his head down so that his eyes are as close as is possible to the ball at the moment of contact. To maintain this focus on the spot without lifting his head, the player must concentrate hard. This can be helped considerably if the player calls out "sweet" as he starts the shot and "spot" on the moment of contact!

Follow through

Is the last part of any shot and if correctly done ensures accuracy. In golf, tennis and cricket it is the same. The eyes of the player must remain where the ball was until the follow through is completed. The player controls the stick so as to take the stick head at least as far as the aiming point. The player uses his brain methodically and imitates a computer. This method can be of assistance. Look at the target—look at the sweet spot—think of a target location. Send a message to the back of the right hand—hit the sweet spot allowing the right hand to obey the message by completing the follow through.

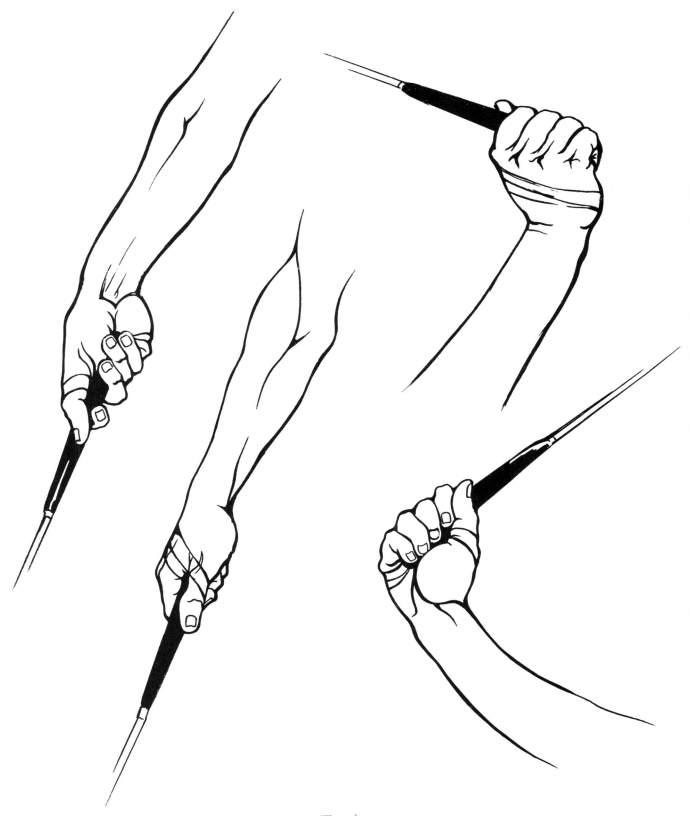

The grip

Chapter 3

TACTICS "A"

Before any individual plays his first chukka, if he expects to acquit himself well, he should know two sets of rules. Firstly, a proper understanding of the laws and penalties of the game is a vital requisite. The only way to comply with this demand is to read the rules in consultation with an expert. The Hurlingham Polo Association rules are included in the Appendices at the end of this book.

Secondly, he should know the rules of his position which, if correctly adhered to, will enable him to contribute effectively to his team. No.1 and No.4 are the two easiest positions to play and beginners should start with one of these. They are similar in several respects and especially because both numbers participate at one end of a line of players.

No.1 is normally the first in attack while No.4 fills the position at the back of the team to ensure a good defence. No.2 and No.3 are in the middle of the line where it is harder to position and anticipate well. As in similar sports to polo, the midfield is the difficult place to play. Hence, No.1 and No.4 are covered in this chapter and No.2 and No.3 are discussed in the chapters Tactics "B" and Tactics "C" respectively.

I have purposely left No.3 to last as he pivots the team and the other three players must first know their own jobs before they can relate to him.

No.1

In most clubs, beginners are automatically put in the No.1 position, yet it can be the hardest position to play, if the other three in the team are selfish. The position is far more important than many teams and players realise. If passes are frequently given to No.1 the opposing No.4 will be forced into a defensive role and prevented from attacking. Instead, many teams tell their No.1, to mark the opposing No.4 as the primary job and very seldom give him a pass. If the opposing No.4 is experienced, he will easily avoid the marking of a novice No.1 and this will enable him to free himself to join in attacks.

Therefore, the primary skill and job of a player in the No.1 position is to be able to receive passes and then carry the ball on towards goal. Furthermore, No.1 should be able to make any shot hit from behind him into a pass that can be then carried on towards goal. In effect, No.1 is the *link between the team and the goal*. To achieve this he needs to be continually adjusting to the play behind him —up, down and laterally. He must ensure that he is close enough to receive a pass of average length and that he is facing in the direction of attack before the ball is hit to him. To do this he must be able to see behind as far as his own No.4 and in front to the left hand goal post. Thus he can have a permanent awareness of the present and the probable future line of the ball. Furthermore he should always extend those two lines to the spot where they should pass him. Then he can move to that spot before the ball arrives. Sometimes this will involve an initial acceleration in the direction of defence towards his own team before a quick turn into attack once more. If his anticipation of the spot was more or less incorrect, a further slight adjustment will take him to the line of the ball. Through this process he should arrive at the line of the ball before anyone else and thus proceed along the line to make a strike without any danger of committing a foul. You could say he is on the main road and unmarked. He will also give himself an easy shot by virtue of the fact that he is following the ball and is not coming to it at an angle. If he sees an opponent on the line of the ball behind him he can and must effect a ride-off before making the strike.

Once the art of linking to goal has been learnt the secondary skill required is to do it at sufficient speed. This means that a No.1 should move fast enough so as not to delay in any way the other three of his team behind him. It is better to miss the ball rather than slow up your own team. At least the opposing

No.1's correctly positioned. No.4's badly placed

No. 4 will be drawn to mark you and the next member of your team can freely battle against any would-be marker for the strike. On the other hand, if you can take the ball on without slowing the game it is even better. This can be called *giving your team velocity*. The ball travels faster than a pony can and therefore should be kept on the move. Many calls by a player to "leave it behind" are incorrect, especially if the No. 1 can hit the ball without slowing up his team and without being marked by an opponent then or in the next few seconds. It is similar to a line of stationary cars at a red traffic light. When the lights change to green the velocity with which the line of cars will move forward is entirely dependent on the first car. The fury of a driver who is in a hurry and somewhere in the line behind is similar to a team-mate behind a slow No. 1.

The third job for a No. 1 is *to mark the opposing No. 4*. This should be attended to immediately his team goes into defence for more than a few seconds. In this situation the opposing No. 4 will probably close up a little to his No. 3, ready to carry on any attack if the ball is presented to him. An early close, i.e. a ride-off that maintains control, by the No. 1 on the opposing No. 4 is the best way to accomplish this. If the opposing No. 4 realises what is happening he may well drop back again. In this case a good No. 1 will revert more to the job of link, looking for the start of any counter-attack by his team. Yet he will keep the opposing No. 4 in view so that a further ride-off can be effected if required. However this job of marking in defence can be greatly reduced if the other two jobs of linking to goal and velocity are accomplished. Even when the ball does not reach him, by being in the correct link position, the opposing No. 4 should be occupied in containing him rather than joining the attack. Marking in attack will only be necessary if the No. 1 fails to achieve his job of linking. Then he will have to mark so as to prevent, impede, or depreciate the backhand from the opposing No. 4.

Fourthly a No. 1 must do all in his power *to keep the ball in play*. Basically this means that he should not shoot wildly at goal whenever he has the ball. Unless he feels highly confident of scoring he should *not* attempt difficult angle shots at goal. Instead he should continue to link the ball towards goal probably placing the ball for another member of his team. More often than not this is best achieved with an angled backhand. In effect this is a continuation of the job of linking. It is emphasized separately to avoid useless shots that cross the back line giving possession to the other team at the ensuing hit in. Occasionally inaccurate shots come from a player behind No. 1 who, through anticipation and adjustment, can prevent the ball crossing the back line with a backhand or by blocking the ball with his stick or pony.

If a No. 1 carries out these four tasks in the order of priority, as given, he will become a highly effective member of his team. Whether he personally scores goals or not is not important. If he successfully provides the link to goal and completes a run by scoring it is most acceptable. But if he frequently misses the goal it is highly unacceptable as he is wasting the work that is being done behind him. But he will only contribute a little if his team seldom include him in their plans for attack. It will mean that they have reduced their effective strength to three-and-a-half players or even less. He will become disillusioned, lose enthusiasm and give less and less as the game proceeds. He will also inevitably come back amongst his team to look for the ball. This will upset the rule of "four players in four positions" and cause a muddle in the team tactics.

Therefore a No. 1 is a vital member of a polo team. To operate well he needs three players behind him who want to, and can, feed the ball regularly to him. He will then be able to carry out his four jobs:-

1. Link to goal his team.
2. Give his team velocity.
3. Mark the opposing No. 4.
4. Keep the ball in play.

If successful, he will enormously strengthen the attack of his team, and at the same time, depreciate the attack of their opponents by keeping their No. 4 busy in defence. And most

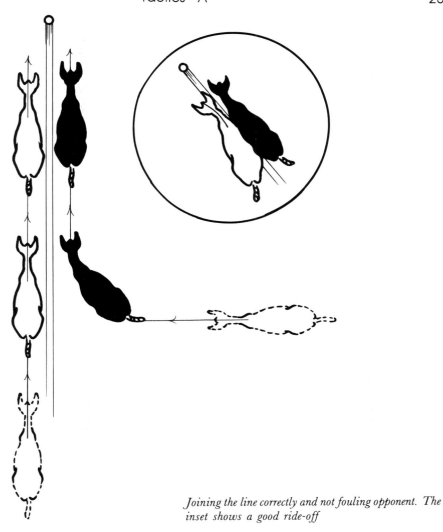

Joining the line correctly and not fouling opponent. The inset shows a good ride-off

important of all he will really enjoy his polo.

The British Army of the Rhine sent a team to Sotogrande in Spain to play two matches in the late 1960s. Playing at No.2 there was a fast, big-hitter, but one whose accuracy was doubtful and who thus seldom gave good passes. Peter Vickery, positioned at No.1, being more accustomed to play back, was more than a little nervous about his task. As captain and No.3 I trained Peter with long

sessions of *exercise one*—receiving passes. Many passes were deliberately put well to one side of him. Looking behind him all the time he had to join the line very early before proceeding to hit the ball. He became quick and good at doing this. In the matches played at Sotogrande he duly made every shot hit by our No.2 into a pass. Even those strikes that went near the corner flags were joined by him before our No.2 himself could get to them. In

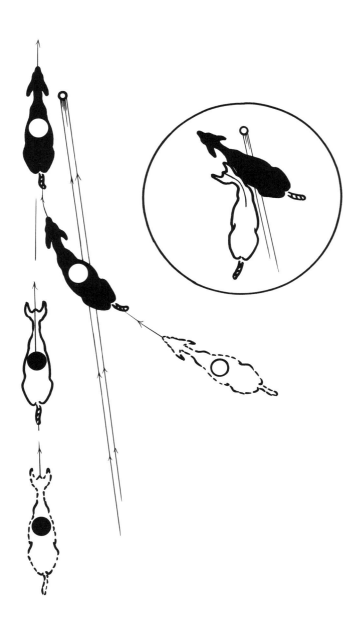

Crossing the line. The inset shows a bad ride-off

fact our No.2 never hit a ball twice in succession. We won both matches. Peter enjoyed them enormously and I will never forget the expression on the face of our No.2. I don't think he could understand what was happening although everything was clearly going well.

The Queen's Royal Irish Hussars had a team all of whom played off a one-goal handicap. In 1968 I coached them for the British Army of the Rhine Captain's and Subaltern's Tournament. After two short lessons their No.1 understood the principle of linking to goal and could put it into practice. In the tournaments he surprised their opponents by the amount of times he achieved possession of the ball and threatened their goal. His contribution enormously improved the effectiveness of the team and helped them to win the tournament against teams of higher handicap.

No.4

This should be the easiest position to play. The No.4 has the most time to watch the game unroll and anticipate what will happen next. Yet the beginner is seldom put in this position because he is expected to have a weak backhand and this is thought to be disastrous.

In fact the offside backhand is normally the easiest shot to teach. Even if the beginner has not learnt to backhand, he can still be effectively used to mark and cancel out his opposite No.1 or the first man coming through in attack. This is considerably easier to do than to carry out the duties of a No.1. I describe it as the task of *shutting the back door*. There are four main rules which, if obeyed, will enable anyone to achieve his task successfully.

Firstly the No.4 must, for the majority of the game, be the last man on the ground. This means that there should be no other player between himself and the goal which he is defending. However there is one important exception to this rule. The exception will apply if the opposing No.1 is of absolutely no value to his team. Maybe he lies too far up the ground where he will never receive a pass or

he is unable to control his ponies. And lastly he might be incapable of hitting the ball in a manner to present any danger to the goal being defended. Then the No.4 can afford to ignore the opposing No.1 and be the last player on the ground out of the remaining seven players. In fact he will take a very small part in the game if he stays behind an opposing No.1 of no value.

Secondly the No.4 must only commit himself to the attack when he sees that he has a forehand shot which he is certain to hit. This means that he is confident of the strike without any interference. If an opponent attempts to ride him off he must know that he will win the ride off before he arrives at the ball. I call this *only going for certainties in attack*. If he thinks that he will lose the ride-off or, if during the ride-off he *feels* that he is losing, then he must stop. In this event the opponent should do one of three things. Attempt a backhand and miss, backhand straight behind him to where the No.4 has stopped or backhand the ball out to the side at an angle. If he does either of the first two, the No.4 will then have an easy and certain forehand. If he correctly backhands to the side, the No.4 can join the line of the ball first and then himself hit a backhand. But if another opponent is already on the line of the ball the No.4 will have to ride-off before hitting his backhand.

Thirdly a No.4 should have an immediate and automatic action if and when he fails to carry out the "certainty" rule as explained above. This can happen because he forgets the rule or that he unexpectedly loses in the ride-off at the last second. Also he might simply miss the ball with an air shot or because someone hooks his stick by surprise. In any event his reaction should be to detach himself at once from the game, the ball, or any opponent and place himself between the ball and the goal which he is defending. I call this *cutting out of the game*. Naturally it involves an 180 degree turn and a rapid move towards the goal during which he must be looking around him at the game. He can thereby quickly correct his mistake and place himself to shut the back door. Furthermore should defence

No.1's badly positioned. No.4's correctly placed

now switch into attack he will be perfectly positioned to back up his team and assist if he can find a certainty to go for.

Fourthly, in defence, he must close to and ride-off the first man through from the opposing team. Normally it will be the opposing No.1 but on occasions it could be any of the other three opponents. This *marking* should be done as rapidly as possible regardless as to who has actual possession of the ball. Thereby the remainder of his team can react more rapidly to mark the other three opponents correctly and possibly launch a counter-attack through a well placed backhand.

If the No.2 and No.3 know that their No.4 will continually shut the back door, they will be able to concentrate on dominating the midfield. Also if the No.4 knows that he is trusted and will *not* be helped with his task, unless badly out of position, he will quickly learn from his mistakes how to improve on, or even perfect, the task. The five general tactics principles are fundamental to the success of a No.4 in being able to shut the back door. It is easier for him, than from any other position, to watch the game with all round vision, continually adjusting to stay in his position from which he can easily close and turn as required.

When training the Irish Hussars team in 1968 I found their No.4 quickly learnt the method of shutting the back door. In the tournament he successfully rode-off whoever came through first in attack. Quite often it was the best player in the opposing team who was so surprised that it affected his overall positioning and influence on the game. This successful contribution by the No.4 combined with that of the No.1, *as already mentioned*, meant that the Irish Hussars were continually spread out in their four positions. The effect of this was a secure defence which greatly assisted the launching of attacks leading inevitably to goals scored and matches won.

Chapter 4

POLO RIDING "A"

To carry out the schooling and exercises which are explained in this chapter it is easier if a riding school or an enclosed area are used. Otherwise go into a field and mark out a square or oblong area with flags, coats or anything else that will stay in position.

Whether you are working in a group or on your own it is equally important that the five main principles of "how to get there" are uppermost in your mind before you start and throughout. You should frequently check yourself to see that you are applying them correctly. The exercises are designed to give you a quiet and effective control of your pony. Each one simulates a movement that will be done by you and your pony at some time during a game of polo.

Remember that without your pony you could not move around the polo ground at all. You should have a healthy respect for, and a good understanding with, all the ponies you play so that you never abuse them. The following schooling movements will assist in achieving this.

THE TIGHT CIRCLE

Let us say that you are riding around the school in a clockwise direction. To make a quick full circle of 360 degrees and then continue around the school as before without losing momentum requires what I call *a tight circle*. The best way to achieve this is to look at your pony's tail first by turning your head right so that you can see the tail over your (right) shoulder. Almost simultaneously, your shoulders, hips, and fork should also turn to the right. This movement by your head and body will swing the pony to the right and into the circle. Then, by keeping your eyes on the tail, and neck reining to the right with a smooth and firm movement of your left hand to your right knee, the circle can be tightened into the shortest way through 360 degrees. If

you lose momentum by circling too tight the pony will come to a standstill or·even start going backwards. This can be avoided by slightly enlarging the circle as you feel the momentum being lost, at the same time your left leg should be poised to kick so as to regain the lost momentum. Many people need to practise continually so as to be able to keep their eyes on the pony's tail throughout without lifting their head. If this happens to you then you might repeat the circle and repeat it again until you completely overcome this problem.

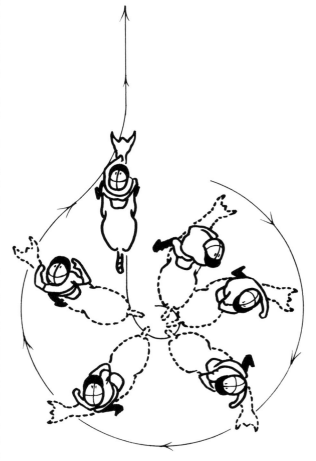

The tight circle

The tight circle should always be done inwards, towards the centre of the school. When you are going anti-clockwise round the school the procedure is exactly the same as above except that you turn the head left to look over the left shoulder and your left hand neck reins to the left knee. The right leg is poised to kick.

Like all riding school exercises the tight circle should be perfected at the walk before you try it at the trot and then at the trot before the canter is attempted. The end product should be a combination of rider and pony that can tight circle to both right and left at a fast canter. Once you have achieved this you will have demonstrated complete control in a movement which is double that normally required in a polo game. Only if you first turn the wrong way might you require to swing more than 180 degrees in a game. Otherwise it is possible to use the 360 degree of a tight circle to adjust your position on the ground in relation to the other players. It could allow you to remain mobile on the (same) spot without fighting with the pony's mouth. If this kind of extreme adjustment can be accomplished it should follow that any minor change of direction or position will never present any problem. Therefore, the tight circle embodies many aspects of polo pony schooling and should enormously assist you in schooling yourself to be *outside your pony*, to use your weight in the direction you are going and to neck rein avoiding contact of your hands on the pony's mouth.

OUTWARDS TURN

This is a turn of 180 degrees and should always be done outwards towards the perimeter of the school. When going clockwise the turn is started by the movement of the rider's body to the left. You should complete the full turn of your body with your eyes firmly fixed on something behind you, before you start to turn the pony. This is important so that it trains you to see behind you before turning. You must not, as in the tight circle, look at the tail but a foot above it and on your fixed point behind you. Ideally, look at the

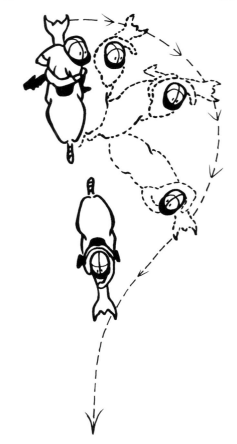

Outwards turn, "look and then turn"

rider behind you or pick an object which is in an equivalent position. Once this focus is achieved then your left hand carries out a neck rein movement to the left and the pony makes one quick positive movement into the new direction, aligning its position to that of yours to look in the same direction as yourself. When going anti-clockwise the outwards turn is executed to the right with the same two distinct movements firstly by the rider and secondly by the pony.

It is a very good exercise to do a series of tight circles and outwards turns mixed up together. For example you are going clockwise and do a programme as follows:-

tight circle — to the right
outwards turn — to the left
a few paces then
tight circle — to the left
outwards turn — to the right

Once again it is vital that you do this combination well and smoothly at a slow pace before you attempt it at a speed.

CROSSING THE SCHOOL

This is most effective if you are working in a group although you can do it by yourself in between tight circles and outward turns. While riding around the school you maintain a constant distance between the ponies, such as one pony's length between nose and tail so that you all fit on one side of the school. One of you should be in charge. Then, on a given command or signal, you can all cross the school together, as if you are one person. This means that ideally you all leave the side of the school together, stay in a straight line *abreast* all the way across and change back into a line ahead at the same moment as you all arrive on the far side of the school. You remain on the same rein and go in the same direction unless otherwise instructed to change the rein by command or signal.

If any one crosses the school too quickly or too slowly the constant distance between ponies will be temporarily lost. This can be quickly and simply corrected by those at fault without a violent change in pace or pull at the pony's mouth. To close up you come away from the side of the school and take a short cut across the next corner. To fall back you neck rein the pony firmly against the side of the school and (go right) into the next corner. These adjustments not only enable the schooling to go more smoothly but also give you good practice in making minor alterations of position in a game of polo. By being outside your pony you can continually see the requirement for adjustment and thereby normally avoid the necessity for any major correction.

JOINING THE LINE

The riding school or area in which you are training need not have any lines drawn in it. But there should be a flag or a prominent object at the centre of each end of the school. An imaginary line from one flag to another would make a centre line dividing the school into two halves. You must always know exactly where that line is although you cannot see it. Just as the good polo player always knows the line of the ball by looking from where the ball was last hit to its present location.

This movement will be explained as if you are schooling in a group although it can also be done when by yourself. On the command or signal to join the line you should ride in by the quickest route to that line. First pick up that line by looking from one end to the other with a quick and smooth turn of your head and body. Then neck rein into that route, looking left and right so as to conform in a line abreast with the group which should arrive at the line together. On arrival at the line the whole group again neck reins in the same direction as before to be line ahead while going along the line. For example, if you are going round the school on the left rein anti-clockwise you will leave the side of the school by neck reining to the left and join the line by neck reining to the left again. Once on the line you must swing your body so as to look forward and backwards on alternative strides. This will enable you to conform to the group and the line, and to see the signal or hear the command "away" which tells you to leave the line and return to the side. Once again you should make an immediate neck rein to the left and head at right angles from the line back to the side. En route, look left and right to conform to the group and on arrival at the side neck rein again to the left to be once more in a line ahead on the side of the school.

If you are on the right rein the whole exercise is done by neck reining to the right throughout. It is an exercise which makes you practice great accuracy in joining a line, and in relating yourself to other people, on a polo ground. Once again you must perfect it at a slow pace before doing it at speed.

You are now in a position to mix up the

four exercises into a series of movements such as starting on the left rein, tight circle, cross the school, join the line and away, outwards turn (now on right rein), tight circle, cross the school, join the line and away, outwards turn (on left rein), tight circle, cross the school and change the rein, join the line and away, cross the school and change the rein, join the line and away and outwards turn.

Inside the pony

Chapter 5

STRIKING "A"

Ten shots will be covered in the following chapters. These will be described in four stages—striking "A", "B", "C" and "D"—together with stick and ball exercises which employ shots and tactics which have been explained beforehand.

Five of the shots described are on the offside and five on the nearside of the pony. Six of the strokes involve hitting forwards and four hitting backwards, known respectively as forehands and backhands.

The right hand grip on the handle of the polo stick can be the same for all the ten shots described. Alternatively, it can be changed for the offside backhands and the nearside forehands by putting the thumb vertically up the handle.

We shall begin by describing striking "A" in this chapter.

OFFSIDE FOREHAND STRAIGHT

There are many different ways and facilities which can be used to teach all the shots in polo. If available, the best is the wooden horse followed by stick and ball on a pony. The wooden horse allows you to experiment and break up into departments the position of the body and the swing of the polo stick. The pony then helps you to finalise the technique with the extra dimension of having to place the pony to the ball. The offside forehand is the shot most used by all players at every standard, but the majority of players are not consistently accurate and seldom achieve an exact straight shot. Normally the reason for this is failure to carry out correctly one or more of the five basic rules for striking. The best way to teach all the shots is to relate to them the basic rules as they apply, so let us begin with this shot.

Placing the pony to the ball requires you to come very straight facing the target you are aiming at. The ball should be about at two o'clock in relation to the pony, two feet to the right of your pony's off foreleg and should be hit before that leg has passed it.

The stick should be held vertically above the hand which is in front and slightly right of your right shoulder. Your elbow should be touching your side in a relaxed manner. This enables you to swing the polo stick back and forward in the same straight plane. If your hand holds the stick inside and left of the shoulder it will have to swing back in a circular plane. This can easily prevent the forward swing from being straight and cause inaccuracy. The best players start with the stick head down near the ground instead of vertical. With the excellent timing that they have developed they will use the lift of the stick as the first movement of the shot and thereby increase the total swing. Others who wish to

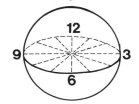

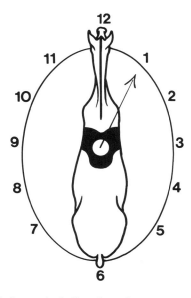

The clock: on the ball and on the pony

copy this will find that it will make them hit the ball late and that the extra swing increases their inaccuracy.

The shoulders (are used to) swing through 90 degrees from being straight on to being parallel with the length of the pony. This is a similar action to drawing the bow when firing a bow and arrow. The right hand will start the swing by going straight back behind the right shoulder and the left shoulder will finish pointing at the ball. This movement can be assisted by the legs and hips swinging underneath the shoulders. Individuals should experiment to find the best way of doing this. Some may prefer the sequence of shoulders, hips, legs. Others may like to revise it into legs, hips, shoulders. In either case the feet should finish up pointing to the right and at right angles to the pony. The bottom of the right thigh and top of the left thigh will temporarily form the fork position on the saddle. The heel of the left foot can maintain your security, if required, by lifting up and forming a brace with the stirrups and leather.

The head moves with the shoulders and then goes down towards the ball. The eyes focus on the sweet spot which for this shot is at six o'clock in the middle of the back of the ball. The hand guides the polo stick so that the middle of the stick head strikes the sweet spot. The follow through should go straight on from the ball to the target and on past it in the same plane. The back of the right hand will guide the polo stick as directed by the mind, but not by the eyes which should remain where the sweet spot was at the moment of contact. This is the same as golf, if the eyes lift immediately to follow the flight of the ball there will be a mis-hit — or even a complete miss, known to most as an air shot.

To perfect the shot it must be practiced quietly and smoothly using little arm strength. This will allow the swing, the strike of the ball and the follow through to be very accurate. Extra strength interjected by the arm will be apt to set up errors and exaggerate any inaccuracy that was already there. In fact the swing is such a big one that, correctly executed, it will dispatch the ball a considerable distance without the use of any extra strength.

If you find that you continue to be inaccurate with this shot you must check your follow through. This can be done by freezing with your right arm and polo stick held absolutely still at the end of the follow through. Then gently lift your head to look at the head of the polo stick and see where it is pointing. Alternatively ask a friend to watch you strike a ball and judge if your follow-through is straight or not. If it is not you should then do several dummy shots, without a ball, until you are satisfied that this follow through is straight. Then return to hitting a ball and recheck the follow through.

On the wooden horse perfect the shot with a stationary ball before trying to hit a rolling one. On a pony start at the walk before speeding up to a trot and on to a canter.

OFFSIDE BACKHAND OPEN

This should be the easiest of all the shots and normally it must be hit at an angle and not straight behind you. Beginners tend to find it harder than the forehand and to hit it continually straight behind them. The result is that the ball either hits a pony that is (straight) behind them or is met by an opponent who is following (behind) them. In any event it will not be a good pass for a team mate who is positioned behind them.

A small swing is adequate and is easier to control. But inexperienced players will copy the stars in making large swings incorporating some kind of winding up process. This causes them to hit late or miss and gives them no chance to direct the ball at the required angle. The five basic rules of striking relate as follows.

The pony is placed so that the ball may be hit early and in front of the forelegs if you want to angle the ball away and out from the offside of the pony. It will help you if you initially approach the ball facing it directly in front and between your pony's ears. When at least five yards away neck rein the pony's head to the left a little so that you now see the ball in front of your right foot. You must then

Offside forehand straight

(Opposite page) *Stick and hand position*
(Left) *Shoulder*
(Below) *Sweet spot*

Offside backhand open

Opposite page left) *Stick and hand position*
Opposite page right) *Shoulder*
Below) *Sweet spot*

hit the ball in front of your foot between one and two o'clock in relation to the pony.

The stick is held vertical with your right hand in front and just left of your head. You will notice that this will greatly shorten the total time taken in executing the swing and assist you in hitting early.

The shoulders swivel away from the ball to the left until your right shoulder is virtually pointing at the ball. Your right hand initiates this movement by going to touch the point of your left shoulder. From there the swing starts with your shoulders returning to the right and the right hand going towards the ball.

Your head goes down to focus on the sweet spot, which is between ten and eleven o'clock. Almost simultaneously the swing arrives at the ball with the centre of the stick head connecting to the sweet spot.

The follow through is carried out by the back of your hand in the direction that the shot is aimed. Once again your eyes must remain where the sweet spot was at the moment of contact.

To perfect accuracy and correct mistakes the same procedures as for the forehand can be used. The stationary ball and the pony walking must be used initially and then returned to whenever any problem with the backhand is encountered.

EXERCISES

Stick and ball is a good way to practice the various shots. But it is not sufficient preparation by itself for your first chukka. Combining with one or more other players in various exercise movements is an excellent way of training. It allows you to experience the pressure of other people relying on your shots, besides giving you practice in sending and receiving passes and co-ordinating with other players.

Once you are able to hit the offside forehand and backhand reasonably correctly you can start doing the first two exercises which I teach. They are both designed to give you practice in sending and receiving passes, while observing all the rules for tactics, polo riding and striking. In this way you can be close to the feeling of actually playing although there is no opposition. In fact, it is a good idea to perfect tactics without opponents to upset you, before trying them against another team. It is surprising how difficult it is to succeed with a simple manoeuvre even when there is no opposition. I am convinced that all beginners and inexperienced players will doubly benefit from these exercises if they can make themselves commentate their actions throughout. Therefore I will suggest the wording for the commentary and you can use it or modify it to your own taste. You can save time by doing the exercises on foot with mini-polo sticks before using ponies. This will help you to remember the format of the exercise and to overcome any inhibitions about commentating your actions out loud.

Joining the line to link to goal

Two players work together. Let us call them A and B. A gives a forehand pass to B who joins the line.

A: "Aiming at sweet spot — keep my head down."

B: "Adjusting, look behind me, join the line."

Now B hits a short forehand and then goes by the ball, leaving it behind him, and heads in the direction of the left hand goalpost. A follows at correct back up distance and then repeats the pass.

B: "Aiming at sweet spot, keep head down; go by the ball in the direction of the left hand goalpost, now look back behind me."

A: "Adjust, not too close, not too far back, look at aiming point, sweet spot, head down."

This process is repeated until A and B have taken the ball from one end of the ground to the other end, where there should be a goal or at least an aiming point. Thus B will be practicing the art of linking. On arrival they should turn round so that they can return down the ground with B passing to A. Progression in this exercise is achieved by the pass being deliberately placed to left or right so that a bigger adjustment to join the line is required. Initially A and B should work together at a slow pace and only increase their speed when they are smoothly moving up and down the ground and hitting accurately.

Early turning to receive a backhand

To simulate a typical situation in a chukka where an early turn is required it is necessary to make the ball run an adequate distance in one direction before the backhand is hit in the opposite direction. *A* and *B* work together again in this exercise.

A hits the ball forward, a minimum of 25 yards, ideally with one shot but if it is too weak *A* must take another shot. *B* follows behind *A* continually adjusting to the correct distance in order to receive a backhand pass from *A*.

A: "Place pony, head down, sweet spot."

B: "Adjusting . . . . adjusting."

Now *A* looks to see where *B* is, selects the place to hit the ball and then backhands. *B* adjusts to one side and then turns before *A* hits the ball.

A: "Where is *B*, place pony, head down, sweet spot."

B: "Adjusting . . . . early turn."

B joins the line, hits the ball forward a minimum of 25 yards and then backhands,

repeating actions and commentary which *A* had done earlier. *A* turns to follow backhand, makes rapid adjustment to close up on *B* and then starts making fine adjustment to receive backhand from *B*, repeating actions and commentary which *B* had done earlier.

B: "Join the line, place the pony, sweet spot; where is *A*, place pony, head down, sweet spot."

A: "Adjusting to close up . . . . adjusting early turn."

This process is repeated many times with the forehand shots being aimed in a direction that enables the exercise to flow smoothly. If either *A* or *B* misses a shot, whether it be a forehand or backhand, the other one should then restart the exercise with a forehand.

Progression in this exercise is achieved by widening the angle of the backhand. Later the backhand round the tail and the near side backhand can be used as well. The pace should not be increased to more than a slow canter. The one who has the strike should be prepared to slow up rather than make his partner hurry too much. This necessitates giving an equal priority to knowing the position of the ball and your partner.

Chapter 6

TACTICS "B"

No.2

This is the hardest position to play for two reasons. Firstly, you are almost certain to be marking the best player in the opposing team. Secondly, you are required, more than in any other position, to switch from defence into attack and vice versa frequently and with little warning. Your own No.3 will rely on you to make attacks out of his backhands, cover him if he commits himself up the ground and subdue the opposing No.3, all at the same time. Hence, a No.2 can never draw breath and must work to the priorities given below and attempt to anticipate the play throughout.

I consider that two tasks have equal first priority in general terms but can be separated once various factors and comparisons of the two teams playing are looked at. As already mentioned the good team will often include their No.1 in their attacks. No.2 is obviously the initial link who can give the ball to his No.1, especially if passes by the No.3 do not reach No.1.

Therefore, one of these two equal tasks is *to be the link between No.3 and No.1*. But the *opposing No.3* has to be *marked* to prevent him passing to his forwards. How can you decide which has the higher priority? The first comparison is between yourself, the No.2, and the opposing No.3. The second is between your No.3 and the opposing No.3. In the first case the answer is simple. If you are stronger as a player than the opposing No.3, to link is your first task and to mark him your second. In fact, he will have to worry about marking you. But if the opposing No.3 is stronger, then you should also compare him with your own No.3. If the opposing No.3 is stronger than the both of you, to mark him must be your first task and to link between No.3 and No.1 is your second job. If your No.3 is the strongest you will need to weigh up the overall situation and decide which task has

the priority. During the game new factors may change the situation and, therefore, your priority. Basically, if you can succeed in giving passes, linking is first. If you cannot, marking becomes the first so that your No.3 has room made for him to gain possession and then pass the ball.

The third priority for a No.2 embraces the five *main* tactical principles. If he sees his No.3 committing himself dangerously, he must decide to change positions with him, thereby *covering his No.3*. With all round vision he sees the necessity to adjust into the position of No.3 so as to keep four players in four positions. Quite possibly an early turn followed by an early close will perfect this task.

The fourth priority concerns your No.1 and his ability to stay in position and carry out his tasks, or his adaptability to interchange positions with you. You must be *prepared to do the jobs of your No.1*, either because he is out of position or because he interchanges with you. Your No.1 might be out of position for a variety of reasons. Lack of experience, his pony out of control, or because he is very tightly marked are three of them. Whichever it is, it is no good passing to a player who is not there. Therefore, you must yourself become the link between your team and the goal. Interchange of positions will be dealt with later. Suffice it to say that if he takes your position you will have to take his to avoid a muddle and to maintain four players in four positions.

If a No.2 plays with these priorities in mind, and in order, he will greatly assist the rest of his team to stay in position and carry out their jobs. The midfield should be controlled and the No.3 will be allowed full scope to use his skill and experience to good effect. The attacks will have more punch and defence will be tightened.

The commonest fault of a No.2 is to be too close or even on top of his own No.3. This is caused by the instinct to chase the ball which tends to override all other priorities and interferes with the tactical principles. This instinct, if not controlled, will often make you adjust in the wrong direction. The best way to

overcome it is to learn and understand the tasks of a No.3 so that you conform to him instead of muddling him.

THE HIT-IN DRILL

Many teams go onto the ground for an important polo match without any tactical plans. "Play it by ear" is often the reply when someone suggests making some plans. This is probably said because players think that plans involve effort which is boring and limits freedom of expression during the match.

The hit-in is a movement which has many variations and gives an opportunity of gaining surprise against other teams. Tactics used at a hit-in can also be employed in any basic attack and penalty hits from the spot or from the centre of the ground. Therefore, a simple drill with some alternatives for the hit-in can be effective and fun, besides giving a team a fundamental plan for any attack. In fact the hit-in should be used as an attacking movement which could end in a goal.

How do you keep it simple? The player taking the hit-in holds the key to this. He will always be the No.4 in good polo, because all the players are strong hitters and No.3 is more usefully employed inside the ground. In low-goal polo if the No.4 is not fully confident of his hitting, it is better if he allows No.3 to hit-in.

For simplicity's sake, when discussing the "hit-in drill" we shall assume No.4 is employed to hit-in. He must hit-in accurately to a place where another team member can retain possession and make the next strike. Some players complicate matters by pretending to hit in one direction and then try to send the ball in another. This is apt to cause inaccuracy and give possession to the opponents, even though an element of surprise is achieved. It is simpler if the player hitting-in approaches the ball in the direction that he is hitting and the player who is intended to make the next strike produces the surprise. How can he? By being on the move as the hitter comes in towards the ball. In fact all four players should be on the move together. With luck your opponents will be

No. 2's good positions.
No. 3's badly placed

No.2's badly placed. No.3's in good position

only watching the ball and can easily be surprised by a member of your team appearing in a new position. The best way to do this is by starting well spread out and then all converging into line.

A basic example of this is the use of the diamond formation. No.4 hits to the right between No.2 and No.1. The line of the ball made by the hit-in is the objective of No.2, who should anticipate its direction before the ball is struck. Starting on or close to the side line, No.2 moves quickly to his left looking to see if his anticipation is correct. A minor or major adjustment, according to the accuracy of No.4, will then be required for No.2 to join the actual line of the ball. With luck this sudden movement will have surprised the opponents and the next strike will be made by No.2 before he can be marked.

At the same time No.1, who started in front of No.4, will have moved to his right to bring himself in front of No.2 as he strikes. In this way the ball should now pass close enough to No.1 to allow him the chance to join the line with a minor adjustment and thereby go on to make the third and next strike. If No.2 strikes inaccurately to one side what can be done by No.1? By looking behind him whilst on the move (outside of his pony) No.1 will see the mis-hit early enough to attempt a major adjustment to join the new line. With a little luck he will still achieve the third and next strike.

No.3, who started on the left side of the goal, moves across the ground with the goal to his right as No.4 canters in towards the ball. His aim is to arrive behind No.1 and No.2 ready to back up the attack or turn in defence if something goes wrong. In this way all four of the team will have moved together and the diamond will have changed into a line. If successful, the effect will be like "a knife through butter" as No.1, with possession of the ball, links his team towards the far goal.

If the hit-in is to the left the procedure is the same except that No.2 moves to his right while No.1 and No.3 move to their left. The diamond will again have changed into a line after only two strikes, because all four players

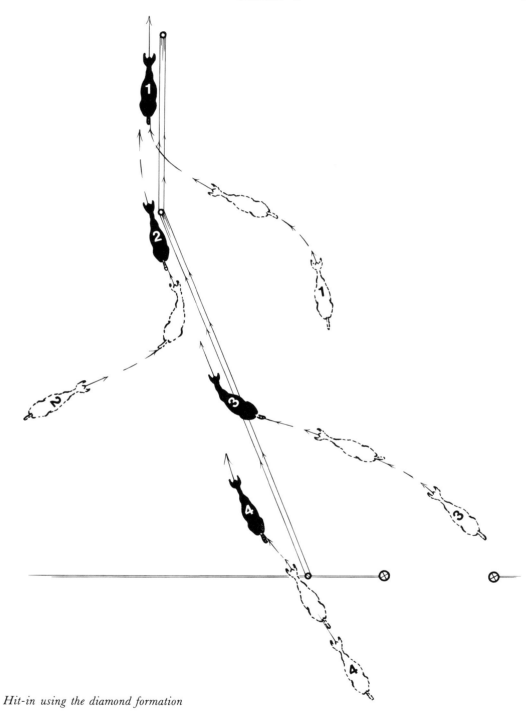

Hit-in using the diamond formation

moved together before the first strike. This is exactly the same as when any attack starts during play and the four players move into four attacking positions by forming a line. No.1 links that line (the team) to goal while the last player is prepared both to back up the attack and defend against any interception or counter-attack by the opponents.

For safety reasons this hit-in for No.2 should be used more than any of the other alternatives in a match. As the ball is struck towards the side line and away from your own goal there is little opportunity for an opponent to intercept and score. No.2 can vary his start position and No.4 can hit to different places out on the side line. A very good understanding between No.2 and No.4 will often enable this variety of length and placing to succeed in a second shot reaching No.1, if he adjusts sufficiently.

The main alternative that can be used, is for No.4 to hit-in across the goal to No.3. This will be much more effective if No.1 knows it will happen and moves towards the centre of the ground instead of the side line. After two shots No.1 can receive the ball and head for the goal at the other end. No.4 must give a signal or a codeword before moving in to hit across the goal between No.3 and No.1. No.3 will have moved as normal before the ball is hit and should only need a minor adjustment to join the line after the ball has passed him. No.1 will have moved towards the centre as No.4 moves in and should be in front of No.3 as he strikes. No.2 will have moved as normal before the ball is hit-in but then he will accelerate to place himself between his No.3 and his No.4 as the team becomes a line down the ground. If No.2 cannot conform in time he will have to adjust and come in behind No.4 to carry out the tasks of a "back".

The key to the success of this hit-in drill is correct anticipation by No.1. So often his adjustment before the ball passes him is insufficient. The result is that he will foul an opponent already on the line as he hits the ball or he will be unable to gain possession. Many players in the No.1 position move straight down the ground, making no lateral adjustment and expecting the perfect pass. If No.2 or No.3 receive the ball and continue down the ground with it, their opponents will have little difficulty in marking them and dispossessing them of the ball. But, if No.1 makes the third shot after good anticipation followed by adjustment to the two previous shots, he should avoid being marked as he continues after the ball. Why? Because his opponents will have conformed to the line made by the hit-in, while No.1 positioned a shot ahead of them. The speed of the ball will have outpaced even the fastest pony of any opponent.

The strategy mentioned above may be successful throughout a match against your opponents. But better players will counteract what is happening by spreading out to prevent the second shot being made by either No.2 or No.3. This will open the way for another alternative.

No.4 hits-in straight to his No.1. A codeword or signal for this will tell No.1 that the hit-in is intended for the open space nearest to him. Instead of positioning for the third shot he will anticipate and adjust to make the second shot. No.2 should attempt to reach a position in front of No.1 to receive a pass from him but if he is unable to arrive there in time he should adjust to come in behind, and backing up, No.1.

The three alternative plans for hitting-in, mentioned above, will only operate successfully if your team is alert. The moment the ball crosses behind the back line giving your team a hit-in, all of your players must proceed to take up their positions without delay. You and your ponies can then have a rest while watching or listening to the appropriate signal or codeword. Then all will see No.4 as he moves and can duly conform as explained. If an opponent appears likely to intervene you should quickly apply the principle of "early close" and possibly take him with you to your next position. But you should not think about this complication until your team can do this drill well without opposition.

PENALTY TAKING

Many players think that everything depends on the man taking a penalty, leaving the rest of the team nothing to do. In fact, there is always a job for each member of the team and it is related to both attack and defence. On occasions the penalty taker will mis-hit, completely miss the ball, or see his shot met by an opponent. Instantly the situation is changed from attack into defence. The striker of any penalty should take care to approach the ball correctly. A common mistake is to circle too close to the ball and arrive unbalanced without knowing where exactly the aiming point is. Even more stupid is to take a penalty when riding a pony that dislikes a stationary ball, especially if there is another reasonably good striker in your team. Naturally the penalty taker ought to practice hitting at the different penalties on each of his ponies at various times between matches. In this way he can find the best pace and appropriate style to effect loft, velocity and accuracy.

Hit from centre or spot

The basic plan should be the same as that at a hit-in. The team should position in a diamond formation with all the players on the move together. The two players on the sides of the diamond should be prepared to take any one of three actions: 1. Receive the ball and pass it on to No.1; 2. back up on the attack made on the other side; or 3. cover the striker if he makes a mistake. No.1 should adjust to whichever side of the diamond the ball will be hit to receive a pass, yet be ready to mark the opposing No.4 if anything goes wrong. The striker should look carefully at the relative positioning of both teams before cantering in to hit. He must select one side of the diamond and then aim for the open space in that area. After hitting he will be the No.4 ready to shut the back door unless he sees another player covering behind him.

There are several alternatives to the basic plan if the team has agreed them beforehand.

60 yards

There are no rules to be obeyed as the team may be lawfully placed anywhere. Yet there is the tactical consideration of four positions to be filled. The striker of the penalty must assume the position of No.4, ready to shut the back door if his shot does not score and the ball stays in play. The No.1 and No.2 should be either side of the goal posts with three alternative actions in mind.

Firstly, to be like the two wings on a jump, thereby helping the near-miss to be redirected through the goal. Secondly, if the ball is going to miss the goal, to stop it before it crosses the back line. Thirdly, being prepared to mark the opposing No.3 and No.4 if their team should regain possession of the ball. The last member of the team will assume No.3 and position himself to the left and in front of the striker. If the shot is strong and not intercepted on the 30 yard line, he joins the line of the ball. But if there is a mis-hit or interception he moves into the No.4 position in order to cover the striker and ride-off the first member of the opposition as their attack develops. Also he must be prepared for the ball to be stopped in the goalmouth and then cleared. In which case he must remain as No.3, adjusting to take the second member of the opposition in attack.

30 and 40 yards

There is only one difference between these two penalties. The rules for them are the same and the suggested positioning of the teams is similar, but one is ten yards longer than the other. The hitter must be in front of his team as he takes these penalties and hence assumes No.1 position. One other player, only, should back up the hitter and naturally becomes No.2 if the ball stays in play. The remaining two players should stay well behind the hitter filling No.3 and No.4 positions. They will mainly think defensively in case there is an interception by the opposition. On many occasions in matches a successful interception has resulted in a goal at the other end of the ground because the players behind the striker of the ball were more intent on attack than defence.

Chapter 7

POLO RIDING "B"

Let us imagine that you are schooling ponies in a group of four or more people. You have already done all the movements described in Chapter 4. The next step, designed to make everyone be even further outside their ponies, is to divide the group into two rides on opposite sides of the school.

RIDE DIVIDES

The instructor or rider in charge can commence this phase when he has the group at the walk, with the first pony approaching one end of the school. He orders the whole ride to go down the centre line. Then he instructs them to number from the front "1, 2, 3" and so on. At the end of the line the odd numbers turn left and the even numbers turn right.

It is now important that 1 and 2 stay opposite each other and conform one to the other throughout. The same applies to 3 and 4, 5 and 6, etc. Inevitably one rider will get ahead of his opposite number from time to time. How can they adjust other than slowing down or speeding up? At the next end of the school the one in front goes deep into his corner while the one behind cuts the corner. At the end of the school each person should pass his opposite number right hand to right hand exactly as and when they come to the line.

All the riders now have at least three others to watch and conform to — the rider opposite them, the one in front or behind and the person who is giving the orders or signals. To do this correctly everyone must stay outside the pony throughout ready to adjust to any signal, change of pace or mistake by any of the others. If anyone looks at his pony his ability to adjust to the remainder will be affected. This is exactly the same as in a game on the polo ground.

Once the riders are correctly positioned on the two sides of the school the instructor can recommence giving orders or signals for the movements described in Chapter 4. For the tight circle all the riders, as before, will circle inwards. Therefore, those going clockwise will circle to the right and the others going anti-clockwise will circle to the left. The opposite applies to the outwards turn. Those going clockwise turn left and the others going anti-clockwise turn right.

When crossing the school all the ponies should be line abreast at the moment that the line is crossed. Here the right hand to right hand rule is not obeyed. Everyone should cross in the correct numerical order. Therefore 2 will pass between 1 and 3 while 3 will pass between 2 and 4 and so on. The highest number will always be at one end and 1 at the other end of the line. After crossing the line everyone should look backwards to see which way the leader will turn on arrival at the side of the school. Inevitably from time to time people will be out of position at the moment when crossing the school begins. A simple method of making an immediate adjustment is to look at the relevant opposite two people and head for the gap between them. Hence 4 should look at 3 and 5 and, regardless of the angle required, aim himself and his pony to pass through the middle of them.

To "join the line" each person should approach it ready to go along the line as a pair with their opposite number. The best way to do this accurately is to look first to see where the line is and then at your opposite number. Then continue to look at each other until you are together on the line. After this all should look round to see the signal for "away". Immediately everyone returns to the side from which he came and automatically continue in the same direction as before duly conforming to the riders at both sides of the school. For some reason many people want to continue to the end of the line before returning to the side. Therefore it may be necessary to repeat this movement of joining the line in pairs several times before it is fully understood.

Each movement should be done at least

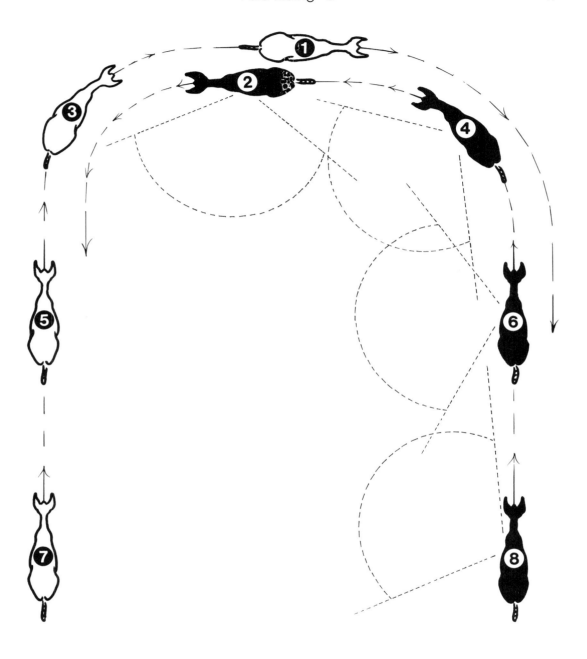

The all-round vision that is required to remain in the correct position throughout the riding school

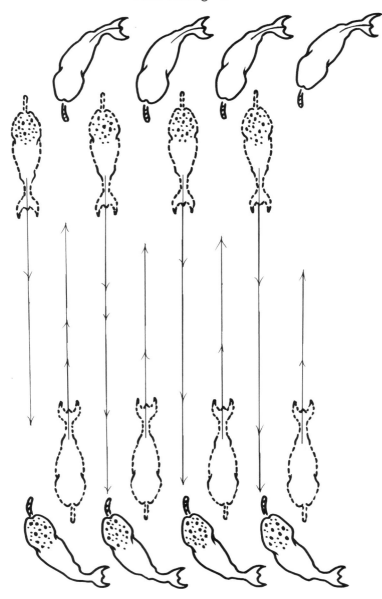

Crossing the school from opposite sides

once at the walk. Then crossing the school should be repeated with a change of rein. After this the tight circle, outwards turn and joining the line are carried out again.

Depending on how quickly everyone learns the correct positioning for these movements a progression through increase of speed can be made. When trotting, whenever you leave the side of the school, if possible, you should sit in the saddle on the fork. Then returning once again to the side of the school you can recommence rising in the stirrups if you wish. At the canter someone is liable to be left behind and the man in charge should not give further orders or signals until this is corrected. If necessary he should slow down to a walk or even halt to make everyone position correctly before the canter is tried again. Perhaps crossing the school will rectify the problem by itself. Thus after fifteen minutes the group working on the two sides of the school should be able to do a programme at the canter, including in it the four movements and several changes of rein. The instructor can take part himself by filling the position of any number. In the beginning he should give both verbal orders and make signals at the same time. As soon as feasible he should cease to call out and only give instructions through signals. This will ensure that everybody has to be permanently outside his pony. All round vision can be further tested by constant changes in pace without verbal orders. This should include some halts. The best time for this is when crossing the school especially after the riders have passed through each other on the line. In this situation another dimension can be added if the instructor first calls out "look behind you" and then halts. Ideally there then should be two straight lines of stationary ponies with the riders looking backwards at each other from one line to the other. Most probably after the first halt in such a situation some riders will look forward

again to see if they have halted. These people will be exposed because their ponies will automatically halt later than the remainder.

Another good testing moment for a halt is when the two sides have just passed each other in line ahead at one end of the school. This is also a good time for an outwards turn.

SUGGESTED PROGRAMME

As a guideline a possible programme for ponies and riders to work on two sides of the school for the first time is as follows:-

At the walk, down the line in single file; from the front number; at the end of the line odd numbers left even numbers right; (the odd numbers are going anti-clockwise and the even numbers clockwise round the school); two or three rounds of the school; cross the school; tight circle; cross the school; join the line; (repeated until done correctly); tight circle; outwards turn; outwards turn; cross the school and change the rein. Now the odd numbers are going clockwise and the even numbers anti-clockwise round the school. Starting with the first cross the school exercise the above programme is repeated.

If everybody understands and performs the programme correctly at the walk it can be repeated at the trot and then at the canter when two or three halts can also be included.

The next step is to delegate to different riders the task of making up their own programme and giving the signals for it. This will make it necessary for the other riders to look in yet another direction so as to see the signals and participate correctly. It will also prepare each individual for schooling his own ponies at home. With just one other person the two can do extensive schooling by working opposite each other taking turns to give and watch all the signals. Naturally a larger group is better. Why? Because there are more people to watch and adjust to.

Chapter 8

STRIKING "B"

NEARSIDE FOREHAND STRAIGHT

This is a shot at which many players are weak and lack accuracy. Why? Because they do not apply the five rules for striking and lose the use of a full swing. In fact it is possible with this shot to give excellent passes and to score many goals.

Placing the pony to the ball is more important than ever so that a full swing can be incorporated. The ball should be between ten and eleven o'clock in relation to the pony at about two feet to the left of the near foreleg and should be hit before that leg passes it.

The stick and hand position should be on the left hand side of the body. The hand ought to be opposite and slightly out from the left hand shirt pocket. The stick should be held vertically above the hand.

The right shoulder turns to the left and points at the ball. At the same time the right hand moves to touch the left shoulder. At this stage the chin should be pressed towards, or even into, the right shoulder over which the eyes are looking at the ball. The shoulders are now parallel to the pony and the right hand is poised to start the swing from a point which is far away from the ball. This movement can be assisted by the legs and the hips swinging underneath the shoulders. The feet should finish pointing to the left, at right angles to the pony. The bottom of the left thigh and the top of the right thigh will temporarily form the fork position on the saddle. If the heel of the right foot is lifted in the stirrup, to be at right angles to the saddle, it will pull the leather tight and secure this fork position.

Now, and not before, the head goes down to make a closer focus on the sweet spot at the same time as the right hand leaves the left shoulder. The sweet spot is at six o'clock on the ball which is in the middle of the back of the ball. The back of the hand guides the stick head to the sweet spot.

The follow through is completed by the back of the hand while the eyes remain where the ball was. The right leg should also stay in position with the heel in the air so as to ensure that the follow through goes exactly in the direction of the target and not to the right of it.

Accuracy can be checked in the same way as suggested for the offside forehand and the calling out of "sweet spot" can be very helpful for this shot. The most important point is that the full swing and not a short wristy shot is made.

NEARSIDE BACKHAND OPEN

Many people find this shot difficult because they do not use economy. Instead they take an enormous swing at the ball with the result that they either miss or strike the ball very late. Others barely attempt the shot from the fear of falling off. The beginner is recommended to use a method which is called "the hammer". To do this he must, of course, place the pony to the ball in exactly the same way as anybody else. It will help if he approaches the ball looking at it directly in front of, and between, the ears of the pony. When at least five yards away he should neck rein to place the head of the pony a little to the right so that he can see and hit and ball in front of his left foot. Here we will deal with the shot that is aimed at a target at seven thirty in relation to the pony. For this the ball should be hit when at ten o'clock in relation to the pony. The hand position is opposite the right hand shirt pocket with the stick vertical above it. Initially the shoulders move away from the ball to the right so that the ball can be seen over the left shoulder. The body weight should be felt in the right leg. At the same time the polo stick is allowed to tilt backwards over the right shoulder like a hammer ready to strike a nail. The right hand remains still combatting the temptation to move to the right and upwards.

The player's head goes down to look at the sweet spot at one thirty on the ball. This is followed by the right hand with a hammer action striking the sweet spot. If you think of or, even better, call out "shoulder, hammer, spot'' it may assist you in applying the technique correctly.

Finally the back of the hand directs the follow through to the target at seven thirty in relation to the pony. If the right leg swivels to the right with the heel upwards the body will be locked on to the saddle in the fork position. This will give the striker security and confidence to be accurate with the follow through in the direction of the target. Thus you will have no reason to be frightened of this shot.

EXERCISES

The hit-in

Can be done by three or four people. It is more constructive for three as this provides increased participation for all. Here it will be explained for three, as before — A, B and C.

The positioning at the beginning will depend on the average length of strike by the participants. Let us imagine that this is fairly weak. Hence A will stand behind the back line so that there is a straight line from him through the ball to the point where the side line and the 60 yard line meet. B is on the side line halfway between the back line and the 30 yard line and C is on the 30 yard line itself in front of the ball.

All three move together. A towards the ball, B across the ground parallel to the 30 yard line and C towards the point where the nearest side line and the 60 yard line meet.

A hits-in with the intention of at least reaching the 30 yard line in the direction of the side line and 60 yard line. B adjusts as necessary and joins the line of the hit-in. C adjusts, and positions, to be approximately fifteen yards directly in front of B.

Calling out the different actions will help, as we saw earlier.

A: ''Look at the target, look at the ball, move, head down, sweet spot.''

B: ''Watch A, move with A across the ground, adjust, join the line.''

C: ''Watch A and B, move with A, adjust to B.''

Now B hits the ball on to C, who joins the line and links to goal with a quiet approach shot. A adjusts to be behind B and to be at the end of a straight line formed by the left hand goal post through C and B to himself, ensuring that he maintains the correct distance behind B. C, aiming at the centre of the goal, takes one or two approach shots, according to what has been previously agreed, and then leaves the ball and heads for the left hand goal post. B and A adjust so as to conform to the line made by the left hand goal post through C, B and A.

A now passes the ball to B who in turn passes to C who approaches or shoots at goal.

B: ''Look at C, head down, sweet spot, conform to left hand goal post and C.

C: ''Look behind me, adjust to B, join the line, look at the goal, head down, sweet spot, head for left hand goal post, look behind me, keep adjusting to those behind me, join line.''

A: ''Adjust to left hand goal post C and B, adjust to B, join the line, head down, sweet spot.''

Unless A, B and C are normally in a team together and wish to stay in the same line out to practise they can change positions for the ensuing hit-in exercises. Thus, at the next hit-in C can hit to A who passes to B. Then at the third hit-in B could hit to C who passes to A.

Interception

This is an extension of the hit-in exercise, where the interception is made by waiting in the middle of the ground as the ball is hit-in. It introduces an opposition and the first thoughts about riding-off. It can be carried out by two against two, three against three or four against four. Let us imagine that there are six people. Three, A, B, C, will take the hit-in. The other three, X, Y, Z, will wait in a row in the centre of the ground. A then hits in from the left hand side of the goal. He hits to B who passes to C. X, Y and Z, in that order are in line abreast at the centre of the ground facing the left hand side line. X and Y allow C to continue past them so that Z can close with him. X also permits B to go past for Y to join him while X himself rides off A.

For the purpose of the exercise A, B, C allow X, Y, Z to control them and gain

Stick and hand position

Shoulder

Sweet spot

Nearside backhand open

(Opposite page) *Stick and hand position*
(Below) *Shoulder*
(Right) *Sweet spot*

possession of the ball. Ideally Z hits an offside backhand angled in the direction of the goal. X and Y "early turn" so that Y can join the line and then pass the ball to X. Z turns to follow X and Y and all three, unopposed, attempt to score a goal. Meanwhile A, B, C do not interfere with X, Y, Z. Instead they regroup in the centre of the ground in a row, line abreast, facing the left hand side line.

X, Y, Z now take the hit-in and are dispossessed in the centre of the ground by A, B, C who return to the goal unopposed and try to score. This process can be repeated several times and then varied. If the hit-in is from the right hand side of the goal by A, B, C then X, Y, Z can start on the right hand side line opposite the centre so that the offside backhand is still used. Otherwise the next progression is the use of the nearside backhand to dispossess the opponents. In this case those waiting in a row will be in the centre of the ground facing the right hand side line.

A, B and C will now call out as in the previous exercises.

X: "Watch A, B, C, allow C and B to go by, look at A, close to A, look at Z, early turn, adjust to Y, join the line, head down, sweet spot."

Y: "Watch A, B, C, allow C to go by, look at B, close to B, look at Z, early turn, look at X, head down, sweet spot, adjust to X."

Z: "Look at A, B, C, look at C, close to C, place pony for backhand, head down, sweet spot, adjust to X and Y."

At this stage if the exercise goes consistently well the instructor could allow one or two minutes of actual play between A, B, C and X, Y, Z to take place. This would start after the first backhand in the centre of the ground. It can be introduced at the end of an exercise session or be used as the method to start the first chukkas that beginners play.

In this way the hit-in is allowed to work without opposition, while the opponents learn how to select and mark the correct man in the midst of play. At the same time by not introducing the formation and tactics normally used to oppose a hit-in the beginner is not taught too much too quickly.

Chapter 9

TACTICS "C"

THE RIDE-OFF

It is guaranteed that if two players of different handicaps engage in a series of ride-offs, in the majority of cases the higher handicap player will win the ball. Why? Because he has the better anticipation which will take him to a position where he will have the advantage. From there he will be the first to see the necessity of a ride-off.

In the polo riding and stick and ball exercises the importance of looking at another man before joining him has been well established. In both cases the actions of the other man were expected and merely needed to be co-ordinated with rather than competed with. Riding-off brings out the extra dimension of competition which itself introduces elusiveness, change of speed and various other tricks. Therefore, to watch an opponent becomes even more important.

The two basic requirements to win a ride-off are:-

1. Adjust to the best position to see your opponent before he sees you;

2. Then do not take your eyes off him until contact is made.

Ball-chasing is guaranteed to prevent you from obeying both these rules. In the world of polo the beginner is told "man first, ball second". This is correct but insufficient. If the beginner does identify the opponent first, while moving towards him he will normally take a glance at the ball. Misguidedly he is trying to time his arrival at both. Where is your opponent going? To the ball. Therefore, if you watch your opponent as you close on him he will take you to the ball. But if you look at the ball your opponent will take it from you or make you commit a foul.

The best way to ride-off an opponent is to place your knee in front of him. This will give you complete control over that opponent. The weight of your pony will be in front of his pony by enough so that you can dominate the proceedings. If you watch his eyes or his hands you should be able to see any deviations from his straight course in time to adjust to it and still place your knee in front.

THE THROW-IN

This is a set piece which happens more than any other. It occurs when a game starts after a goal, if the ball goes out over the side line, after someone is hurt or after any stoppage — whatever the reason. Yet it can cause confusion for beginners and for this reason I teach it after the hit-in. A team needs a good drill for the throw-in if players are to avoid a muddle and succeed in quickly spreading out into the four positions. Therefore the hit-in, where the game naturally opens out, has been explained first.

However, if the team has a drill at the throw-in not only can the game be opened out quickly, but a tactical advantage can often be achieved. The key to this drill is the action taken by No.1 and No.4. If either of them fail to move quickly into their normal positions after the ball is in play there will be a problem of some kind. For example, the back door will be left open or a quick attack will fail giving possession to the opponents because there is no one to link to goal.

At the throw-in the teams should be in a line rather like a "line out" in rugby. Traditionally most teams line up in numerical order although there is no rule that says they should do so. The No.4 will vary his position according to the tactics of his team. Some players will choose to stand last in the line, others slightly behind and at right angles to the line. The former is normal practice in top-class polo.

The umpire throws the ball between the two lines of players who cannot move or touch one another until the ball has left his hand. No.1 should try to hit the ball and follow it. But it is difficult for No.1 to do so and on most occasions he misses and the ball goes past him. This is the only time that a No.1 should not look behind him as that would delay him and might tempt him to ball-chase instead of moving to the correct position. Where should he go? To a position from which he can link to goal if the ball is hit up the ground. The opposing No.1 may also be trying to do the same thing with the result that both could proceed towards the side line locked together without either of them giving way. A simple way to avoid this is to pass behind the opposing No.1.

No.4 must be ready to decide between two actions. To proceed to shut the back door or to go into attack. He should take the decision by asking himself the question: "will the ball come through the line up?" If the answer is "yes" there is a second question. "Is it a certainty?" If the answer to either question is "no" he must move quickly to be the last man and to mark the first opponent. If he has a certainty he ought to pass to his No.1 or temporarily become the No.1. His No.4 position should be filled by the No.3 until he finishes that attack and returns to his defensive duties.

The No.2 and No.3 should compete for the ball. If successful, they should pass to No.1 and follow up one behind the other. If they fail they must rapidly mark the second and third member of the opposing team. The opponents may mount the first attack. But this could be duly stopped by quick marking and then, from a backhand pass, No.1, adjusting to be the link to goal, could turn early, join the line, make an approach shot and then shoot for goal.

THE BARRIER

We have discussed the importance of the four players covering four positions throughout a game. For a team to obey this rule is not as easy as it may sound. There are many reasons why a player can be drawn into the wrong position. The ground is so large, the game so fast and the unexpected happens so often. If we place a barrier in the middle of the four players and have different rules for those on either side of the barrier we can insist that there are always two on each side and the situation will become simpler.

The barrier will move up and down the ground with the play but not necessarily with the ball. The two players in front of the barrier, normally No.1 and No.2 should try to speed up the attacks and hurry the opposing defenders. To do this when in attack they must go for every ball in their area of the ground even if their relevant opponent appears certain to hit a backhand before they can get to it. Thereby the opponent's backhanders should be depreciated through loss of length and/or accuracy and these two players will stay in front of the barrier whatever happens. The process of depreciating the opponent's backhand may be quick or may take time. Either way the aim is to cause the backhander to mis-hit or miss completely. Lack of length or angle will assist your team to regain possession of the ball. Even if this does not happen in the early stages of the game it is very likely that eventually the pressure will get to your opponent before the end of the match. However, it should not be serious if and when a good backhand is struck, because there are two players of your team, usually No.3 and No.4, behind the barrier waiting to receive it. These two do not want their forwards interfering with them. On the contrary they wish to return the ball over the barrier immediately, or in due course, and hope that No.1 and No.2 will then be positioned to receive it.

How do two players stay permanently behind the barrier? Both obey the rule, already given to number 4, that they do not commit themselves to make a forehand shot unless it is certain that they will strike the ball or it is clear that one of the forwards will cover them and take their position if they fail to make the strike. If the forehand is successful hopefully it should send the ball on as a good pass over the barrier to No.1 or No.2. Meanwhile the barrier remains in the middle of the four players. If it is not certain that a strike will be made the players behind the barrier stop, cease to compete for the ball and anticipate where the opponent's backhand will go to. Possession should then be regained and the ball returned over the barrier to the two players who ought to have adjusted in the method previously explained.

If the four players are always aware of where the barrier is, and which side of it they should be, the chance that the four positions are always filled is greatly increased. Inevitably in any team sooner or later a No.3 or No.4 will go forward through the barrier when they should not. Also a No.1 or No.2 will come back through the barrier at the wrong time. But the damage to the team will be minimal if the culprit realises the error in time and immediately adjusts by passing through the barrier again to be on the correct side.

"Cutting out of the game", the rule as described earlier for playing No.4, is the way that such an adjustment ought to be done.

No.3

In the majority of teams No.3 is the best player. The rest of the team should permanently watch him so as to conform to him and be guided by his actions. If No.3 plays his position correctly and in the interest of the team, their anticipation should be improved by adjusting to his every move.

From behind the barrier No.3 is the pivot of his team. He achieves this by obeying the following four rules.

First, in defence No.3 marks the second man of the opponents. Closing to him as rapidly as possible will assist the rest of the team to select the correct opponent to mark.

Second, he is always ready to cover his No.4. He can do this in two ways. Either by taking the position of back, when No.4 commits himself to attack. Or, as an adjustment to his own mistake if he has over stepped the barrier when not covered by one of his forwards. In the latter situation with a quick tight circle he might be able to re-position himself as No.3 behind the barrier with No.4 remaining in his own position at the back but a large circle will invite No.4 to enter into attack with confidence in the knowledge that he is now covered by No.3. In this way No.3 and No.4 can maintain a continual backup to any attacks and yet one of them is always positioned to shut the back

door against a surprise counter attack.

Third, he must not cross the barrier unless covered by another player. In effect this means that in attack, like No.4, he must only go for certainties. If the opponent definitely has possession and is about to backhand, No.3 should stop. If the backhander is weak he can join the line and regain possession. If the backhander is strong No.4 joins the line and No.3 adjusts to him.

Fourth, he distributes the ball to initiate attacks. Accurately angled backhands, setting up interchanges or backing up his forwards with forehand passes are the principle ways of doing this. From behind the barrier he can attempt to keep the ball in front of it so that his forwards regularly receive the ball instead of having to come back to look for it.

By carrying out the four rules No.3 will become an effective pivot. But this may be of limited value if one or more of his team do not understand these rules. For example, on one occasion I was asked to substitute for the No.3 of a team with which I had never previously played. There was no time to discuss tactics. After a few minutes I saw my No.2 stop and allow the opposing No.3 plenty of time to backhand the ball. I duly requested that he should hurry and hustle the opposing No.3 in future. A little later I stopped to allow the No.2 of the other team to backhand because I did not wish to cross the barrier. Suddenly there was a shout from my own No.2 calling me a hypocrite with a four letter word attached to it. Our team was in disarray and it was difficult to be an effective pivot in such a situation.

FACING THE HIT-IN

We have discussed the alternative ways that a hit-in can be made. It was explained that surprise could be achieved through everybody moving at the same time. Now how can these tactics be countered and possession of the ball taken from the team that is hitting in? There are many formations and tactics used by teams in the varying standards of polo. Here two systems will be suggested.

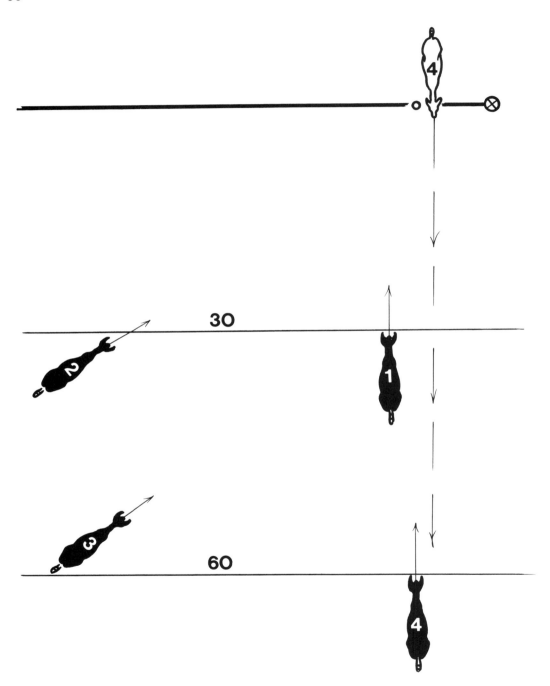

Facing the hit-in from the "box"

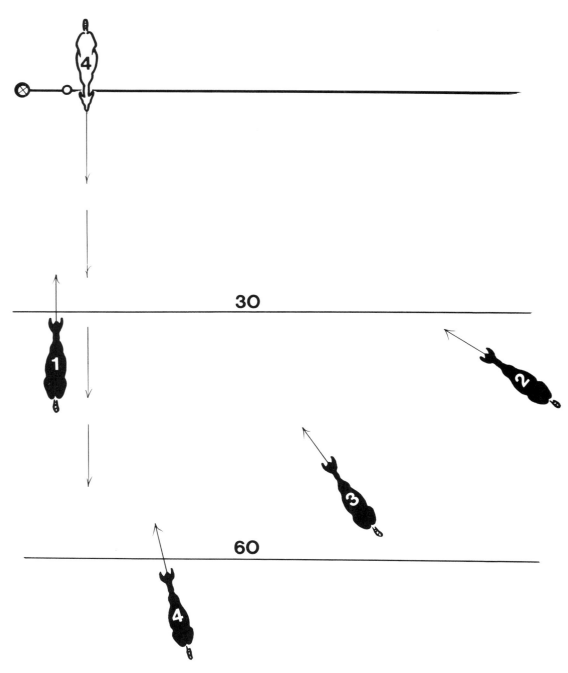

Facing the hit-in with the modification of the "box" in order to meet the ball when possible

Two against one

One good tactic is to position your team so that the opponent who will receive the ball from the hit-in will find himself outnumbered by two against one. The exact positions of your team will depend on the length of strike expected from the hit-in. The formation is called "the box". Your No.1 stands just behind the 30 yard line in the middle of the ground with your No.4 thirty to forty yards behind him. Out near the side line No.2 should be between the 30 yard line and 40 yard line while No.3 is behind him.

If the hit-in is towards the side line the opposing No.2 will attempt to make the second shot. For the short strike your No.2 will be positioned to ride him off after which two alternatives exist. Either they will neutralise each other leaving the ball for your No.3 or your No.2 will hit a backhand to your No.3 who has moved goalwards.

For the long shot your No.2 should release the opposing No.2 so that your No.3 can wait for him and be well positioned to win the ride-off. Again, two alternatives arise as there may be a neutralisation or your No.3 may win the ball to hit a backhand. If the former happens your No.2 will be able to backhand to either your No.1 or to your No.3 if he has turned into attack after the neutralisation. But if the latter takes place your No.2 after an early turn ought to be able to join the line and hit a forehand towards goal.

In the same way if the hit-in is across the goal your No.1 and No.4 will be positioned to operate as two against one to dispossess the opponent who follows the ball. Otherwise your No.4 will continue to obey the rules of his position by ensuring that he is the last man between the play and the far goal. Should it happen that your No.2 and No.3 fail to win possession and the opposing No.1 or any other opponent burst down the line, your No.4 must be there to contain him.

Your No.1 can play an important part whatever happens. If possible he should position to be "stick side" of the man taking the hit-in. This means that with polo sticks in their right hands they would meet stick against stick if they moved towards each other. Thus, in the unlikely event of a very weak straight hit-in No.1 will be able to meet the ball without fouling. For a strong hit-in, No.1 will be able to ride off the hitter as he follows his shot and from this action the No.1 will be well placed to make an early turn if a backhand from your team is forthcoming.

Meeting the hit-in

With a small modification of the box formation the team facing the hit-in can become more aggressive. The possibility that one of the team can meet the ball to score a goal is increased. This is achieved by moving No.3 a little inwards and forwards so that he is equal distance between No.2 and No.4. All three must stand still in their positions in order that the man hitting-in is not presented with an obvious hole through which to send the ball. Now, unless the ball comes on a course that passes exactly between No.2 and No.3 or No.3 and No.4 one of the three may have an opportunity to meet it. How? By adjusting sideways before moving forwards. Any ball within three yards to the left or right of the pony can be met. In fact it will be easier to hit the ball when meeting it if a player waits instead of moving forwards. Why? Because the velocity of the ball will probably be decreasing as it approaches the player.

If it is not possible for anyone to meet, after a small adjustment by No.3, the box system can be made to operate. But when one of the three sees that a meet is possible for him he should call out "meeting". This will tell the others to cover him in case he misses the ball. Therefore if No.2 meets the ball, No.3 and No.4 move towards the side line to be behind the No.2. If he misses they can ride-off any opponent who follows the ball. If he succeeds with the meet they can turn and follow him in a back up position from behind the barrier.

In the same way if No.3 meets he can be covered by No.2 and No.4. This means that No.3 will cross the barrier and No.2 will take his place behind it. Also if No.4 meets he must be covered by No.2 and No.3. This time No.4 crosses the barrier while No.2 goes behind it.

In many teams this tactic of spreading out to meet the hit-in never works because one of the players, normally No.2, will not stay in position. Instead he wanders across the ground to where he expects the ball to come. It is then easy for the man taking the hit-in to find a gap through which to send the ball. But those players who learn to use this tactic successfully not only score goals from it but also learn how to meet a ball during the run of play in any situation.

Chapter 10

POLO RIDING "C"

RIDING IN PAIRS

It is hard enough to be outside your pony in order to have all round vision when riding a pony on its own. For much of a polo match a player is riding alongside another pony whom he is trying to control while seeing what everybody else is doing. Therefore, to be a good player he must learn to be outside "a pair" while retaining control of his opponent.

In the riding school this extra dimension of polo riding can be practised. Earlier we had arrived at a stage where individuals were conforming to riders on both sides of the school while doing the four main school movements. If the instructor waits until 1 and 2 are approaching an end of the school, he can then order all the riders to proceed along the line in pairs. At the end of the line the first pair turn left, the second pair turn right, the third pair left and so on. Now all the riders will have to stay in their pairs while conforming to the pair on the opposite side of the school, the one that is next to them and the leader who is giving the instructions and signals.

Each pair should try to ride together as if the two riders are on one pony. To achieve this you must continually keep an eye on your partner and when looking away at other riders try to feel that his pony is still alongside. If in doubt look at him and adjust as necessary. The rider on the inside must not leave his partner behind when crossing the corners or leaving the side of the school. Instead he should check slightly to ensure that he brings the outside man with him at all times. To adjust to the pair on the other side of the school the same technique as before should be employed. If one pair falls behind they must cut the next corner and the pair that is in front should then go deep into their next corner. At the ends of the school each pair should pass the relevant opposite pair when crossing the line and should be right hand to right hand.

After going around the school two or three times smoothly the leader should signal "cross the school". The pairs pass through each other on the line in numerical order. Therefore the second pair will go between the first and third pair. On reaching the far side of the school the riders must look back to see if there will be a change of rein or not. Immediate adjustments will then be necessary in order to conform accurately to the others.

Next the pairs will be instructed to "join the line". The result should be a smooth transition to being on the line in fours. The outside man of each pair watches his opposite number closely until they are together on the line. The inside man tries to place his partner on the line next to the opposite pair. In the same way as for riding in single file the "away" instruction is given and the pairs return to the side of the school from which they came. Hence the inside man places his partner on the perimeter of the school ensuring that he does not leave him behind.

Now a mixture of crossing the school and joining the line with several changes of rein will keep all parties alert, especially if there is a change of pace and some halts from time to time. But if anyone becomes badly out of position the leader should return to the walk and allow the correct positions and distances between the pairs to be resumed.

How can a pair "outwards turn"? Most people would answer that the riders stay alongside each other as the inside man becomes the outside man and *vice versa*. In fact it is quicker and easier if they turn individually. Also this is a good way to practice the art of marking a better player who is twisting and turning to avoid your attention. Therefore the inside man remains on the inside. The secret is that he should first halt and then wait until his partner is half turned before he himself turns outwards. Throughout, the inside man closely watches his partner in order to achieve the turn and stay as a pair afterwards. If the inside man turns a little late he can adjust to rejoin his partner by cutting the next corner of the school.

A possible programme for people working

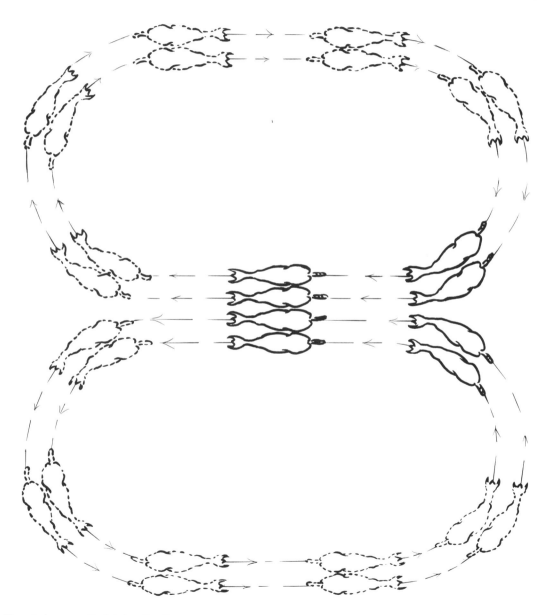

Two pairs correctly joining the line

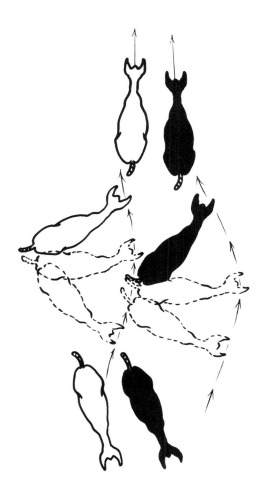

Outwards turn in pairs

in pairs for the first time is as follows:-

At the end of the school down the line in pairs. At the end of the first pair left, second pair right etc. Two or three rounds of the school. Cross the school. Join the line and away. Outwards turn. Cross the school. Outwards turn. Cross the school and change the rein. Now repeat all the above on the

different rein. If this is done at the walk, followed by the trot and then the canter all the pairs should have time to become well accustomed to each other.

Later, many variations can be added including looking backwards followed by a halt.

Chapter 11

STRIKING "C"

THE OFFSIDE FOREHAND CUT

This is a shot which many players find difficult to do at all while others are never accurate with it. Why? Because they use the wrong hand position and try to hit the ball too early. In fact it is a relatively simple shot, using the correct economic technique, and is most effective for giving accurate passes besides sometimes shooting at goal.

When placing the pony to the ball you should approach it on a path a little wider from the ball than for the straight forehand. In relation to the pony the ball should be struck between four and five o'clock.

The best hand position is slightly behind your body. The stick is vertical and thereby ready to be taken the shortest route to be over the quarters of the pony. The fork must turn to the right more than ever before to bring the left shoulder to point at the ball as the right hand draws the bow over the quarters.

The sweet spot is between seven and eight o'clock on the ball. The follow through should go to between one and two thirty in relation to the pony, depending on the exact location of the target. It is more vital than ever that the head remains down until the follow through is completed.

If the above is carried out correctly the ball will barely be cut! Instead the ball will have been dispatched accurately using a straight swing with the utmost economy to the target.

THE OFFSIDE FOREHAND UNDER THE NECK

There are many different ways of hitting under the neck. It is harder to be accurate than many people realise. Why? Because the ball must be struck very early. Therefore the technique that is suggested uses maximum economy and can be modified at a later stage if full confidence is attained.

Place the pony to hit the ball well out in front of the forelegs of the pony between one and two o'clock in relation to it. The hand position is at the end of a straight arm which is pointing in the direction of the ball.

Let us imagine that the target is at eleven o'clock in relation to the pony. Then the bow is drawn sideways and out to a position at about three thirty in relation to the pony with right arm remaining straight. The left leg accentuates the small turn of the fork which moves the left shoulder to point at the ball.

The sweet spot is at four o'clock on the ball with the follow through going to the target at eleven o'clock in relation to the pony. The right arm takes the most economic route and remains straight throughout while the eyes stay rooted to where the sweet spot was. The swing is in a different plain because the elbow is never bent during the shot.

Players often have an opportunity to score with this shot from the right hand side of the goal. Because of the angle the width of the goal is considerably decreased giving less room for error. Therefore the necessity of striking the exact sweet spot together with the correct follow through is more important than ever.

OFFSIDE BACKHAND ROUND THE TAIL

This is a very important shot. Not only does it pass the ball at a good angle across the ground from one player to another but it delivers the ball to the offside of the recipient. This makes it easier for him to keep possession of the ball as it will not be necessary for him to cross the line.

Some players have difficulty in hitting round the tail because they cannot wait for the ball to be in the correct place. As a result they hit the ball too early and it either goes into the pony's legs or straight back for an awaiting opponent to meet.

To place the pony to the ball the player starts by coming a little to the left of the line. As the head of the pony reaches the ball it is allowed to swing slightly to the right towards the ball. Then the pony should continue straight until the ball is just about opposite the

Offside forehand cut

(Opposite page) *Stick and hand position*
(Left) *Shoulder*
(Below) *Sweet spot*

ffside forehand under the neck

Opposite page) *Stick and hand position*
Below) *Shoulder*
Right) *Sweet spot*

Offside backhand round the tail

(Opposite page left) *Stick and hand position*
(Opposite page right) *Shoulder*
(Below) *Sweet spot*

off hindleg and is between four thirty and five thirty in relation to the pony. The ball can now be hit with a simple swing round the tail. The wider the angle between the pony and ball the earlier the shot can be made. The smaller the angle the later the ball must be struck to avoid hitting the pony's legs. Care should also be taken not to cross an opponent who is behind by over doing the angle of the pony to ball.

The hand position is as for all offside backhands at the left hand shirt pocket with the polo stick vertical above it. As early as possible the right shoulder should point at the ball in order to follow it as the pony is going past it. The sweet spot is between one and two o'clock on the ball and the player can focus on this by looking over the right shoulder. The follow through is guided by the back of the hand to the target between six thirty and seven thirty in relation to the pony.

By placing the pony correctly a large straight swing can be made from the shoulder to the end of the follow through. Hence the timing of the shot can be perfected, arm strength is not necessary and the long shot which follows will turn defence into attack.

EXERCISES
Behind the barrier

A and B start at one end of the ground. A passes to B who makes a quiet linking shot towards goal. B then approaches the ball again and simulates missing it which in reality could be caused by a ride-off, or hook or a genuine miss. B follows this with a quick turn and circle to the left or right. This movement should place B behind A who now hits a quiet shot towards goal. A then simulates the miss and turns left or right before circling to be behind B once more.

A: "Look at the target, head down, sweet spot."

B: "Join the line, look at the target, head down, sweet spot: pass over the ball, look behind me, get back behind A."

A: "Join the line, look at the target, head down, sweet spot: pass over the ball, look behind me, get back behind B."

In this manner A and B continue up the ground taking the ball to and through the far goal. They are practising the action, previously described, of "cutting out of the game", as one of the rules for No.4. This provides the team with an ever present back up, a player continually placed to shut the back door and two players always positioned behind the barrier.

Opposing the hit-in by two against one

A hits in to B who is opposed by X and Y. They are standing one behind the other near the side line on the 30 yard line and 60 yard line respectively. It will depend on the length of A's hit-in whether B encounters X or Y. B allows X and Y to dispossess him by employing one of the two methods: One of them neutralises B leaving the ball for the other; or one of them wins a ride off with B and backhands the ball towards the goal for the other to receive.

Both methods should be terminated by X and Y scoring a goal unopposed by A and B.

A: "Look at the target, head down, sweet spot."

B: "Look behind me, join the line, allow opponent (X or Y) to prevent me from hitting the ball."

X: "Look at B, adjust to ride him off or to receive a backhand from Y."

Y: "Look at B, adjust to ride him off or receive a backhand from X."

X or Y: "Join the line, look at the goal, head down, sweet spot."

After this X hits in to Y, who is opposed and dispossessed by A and B who use one of the two methods. A and B then attempt to score a goal unopposed by X and Y. This can be followed by B hitting in to A after which Y could hit in to X. If there is time the instructor should ensure all variations of both methods occur.

Chapter 12

TACTICS "D"

INTERCHANGE

We have discussed the rules for positions in detail. Positions and drills for the set pieces have been suggested. Will this be enough for a team to know before playing in a competitive game of polo? *NO*. The players must also know when and how they can interchange positions without breaking the rule of four players in four positions.

There are three principal situations in which interchange can occur without upsetting the tactical deployment of the team:

1. When two players in the team are facing each other.
2. When all the team are in defence.
3. When all the team are in attack.

Two players A and B facing each other

When the ball is between two players of the same team there is the alternative that the ball could be hit by either of them. A could hit a forehand or B a backhand. Who should take the shot? It depends on the situation. But A with the forehand is wrong to presume that it is his shot. If he does take it the result normally is that his shot does not reach another team player while A and B are temporarily filling one position between them. Why? Because B will now turn up too late to have any chance of receiving the pass and winning the ball against his opposite number. A, while following his forehand, inevitably closes up to B who is completing his turn and proceeding to the new area of play. This means that not only will possession of the ball be lost, but the required positioning for defence will have been vacated.

What would happen if B with the backhand takes the shot? He can angle the ball to the side and away from the expected route of play. Then A, instead of hitting that forehand should have moved to the side and passed B before the backhand is made. Thus the ball

will reach another player, A, who will probably be unmarked. Through the motion of interchange A and B will have kept possession and will have not been together in one position at any time. The opposition should be surprised and their defence will be stretched. If either A or B mis-hit causing their team to change into defence, the positioning will be correct.

All the team in defence with the ball between A and B

This opportunity for interchange often arises through the quick thinking of A or the all round vision of B who calls out "interchange" before making a backhand.

Maybe A has been prevented from hitting a backhand by an opponent, X, thereby leaving a ball between A and B. This gives B a chance to backhand and A has the opportunity to turn up and receive a pass from B.

In a second A and B and their team have turned defence into attack with a good possibility existing that A is unmarked when in possession. Why? Because there is an element of surprise produced by A leaving his defensive task. As a result X is unlikely to go with him. In which case B will now close onto X leaving his opposite number, Y, out of position and unable to mark A. In fact A and B will have interchanged while X and Y will have failed to adjust to this manouevre.

An interesting point is that if A had won the ride off against X and hit the backhand to B it is highly probable that Y would have marked B without difficulty. This suggests that A should be looking at all times for an opportunity to set up this interchange instead of taking a backhand.

A and B could represent No.2 and No.1, No.3 and No.2 or No.4 and No.3 respectively. It is easier for No.4 and No.3 to effect this interchange than the others. Why? Because No.4 (A) usually has more time to read the game than anyone else. Also the opposing No.1 (X) is the least likely to anticipate and interfere with the interchange when concentrating on linking his team to goal.

It is important that A and B are prepared to

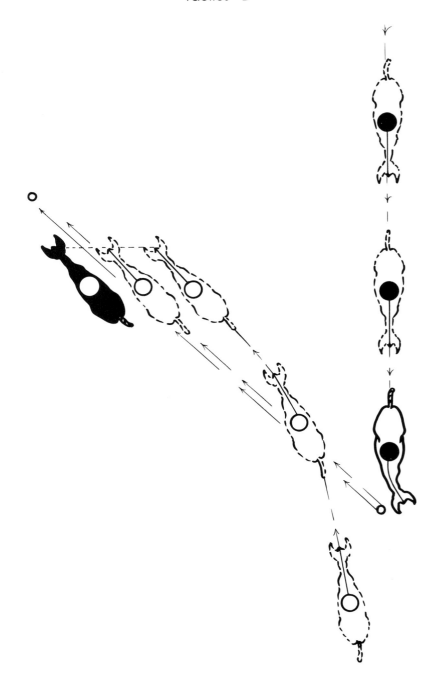

Interchange between two players facing each other — with the ball between them

assume each other's tasks in defence if the movement fails.

All the team in attack with the ball in front of A and B

A would normally hit a straight forehand to another team player or for himself to pursue and hit again. However this is so predictable that on many occasions an alert opposition would prevent the second hit.

If A is near the left hand side line he could pass to B and interchange positions with him.

How? By making a forehand cut shot while B goes past him in the direction of the goal. B must have anticipated the interchange and started goalwards before A takes the shot. B should be careful not to foul when joining the line of the ball. A has to adjust quickly to take over the position and the role of B in order to back up the attack and be correctly placed to defend against any counter attack.

Another way that this interchange could happen is if A is near the right hand side line. By pulling the ball under his ponies neck A

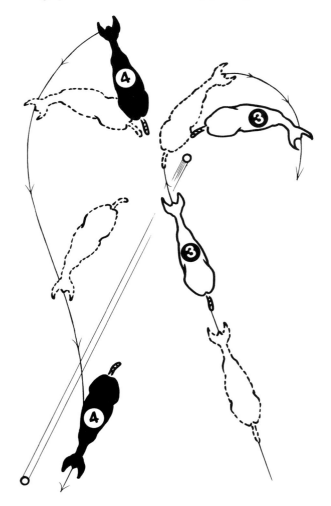

Interchange to turn defence into attack. Backhand from No.3 to No.4

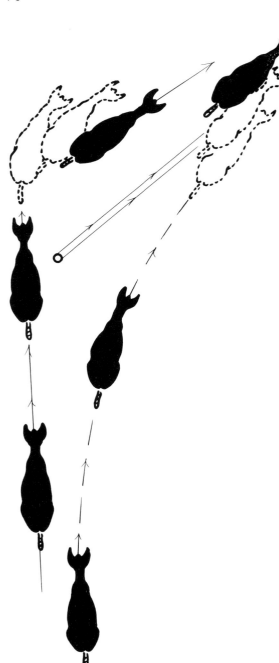

Interchange on the forehand.
Example with cut shot

can provide *B* with the opportunity to overtake him and receive the ball while heading for the goal. *B* will need even better anticipation to succeed with this interchange because to reach the line of the ball he will have that much further to go. Also *A* should adjust even quicker to place himself behind *B* and assume his role.

A and *B* could represent No.1 and No.2, No.2 and No.3 or No.3 and No.4 respectively. No.1 and No.2 are the two players most likely to carry out this interchange. Why? Because they often need such a tactic to overcome tight marking by the opposing No.3 and No.4.

A point of interest is that in both the above two examples if *A* had successfully pursued the ball for a second shot, instead of interchanging, he would probably have committed a foul. How? At speed after hitting a forehand cut or neck shot *A* will leave the new line of the ball. If he then gallops direct and by the shortest route to the ball and there is an opponent behind him *A* will cross and foul that opponent as he makes the second shot. Therefore *A* must first rejoin the new line or ride off that opponent who is behind him unless he sees that *B* as overtaken him. This interchange not only produces surprise, but also speeds up the pace of the attack while lessening the possibilities of a foul.

Besides learning another way of interchanging it should now be clear that it is possible to foul by crossing the line of the ball even though you are following your own shot. The anguished cry of, "Oh! No Umpire, I hit it last", is a demonstration of considerable ignorance. It is surprising how often such a cry is heard on the polo ground. Sometimes it is said by a player with a handicap or with such experience that he should know better.

These three ways of interchanging positions are relatively easy to explain and even demonstrate. But in the beginning it is nearly impossible to make a team of all low-goal players set them up and carry them out. Why? Because the instinct to ball-chase over-rides the necessary tactical thinking required to operate these interchanges. The player nearest to the ball always wants to hit it regardless of the consequences. If he has a forehand he often tries to hit to where he might have a second successive shot.

To overcome this disease of ball-chasing it is necessary for an instructor or team captain to set up interchange situations in practice chukkas or to make the team do interchange exercises often. Much time can be saved by practice on foot on the mini ground.

RECOVERING GROUND

When any player makes a mistake which gives the opponent he should be marking an advantage there is a simple remedy that can be used to recover any ground lost. An example is seen where a No.4 (A) turns in defence too late to find the opposing No.1 (X) has gone past him. The back door is open giving X an opportunity to approach the goal and then score.

An inexperienced A will chase X trying to catch up by galloping faster than him over the same ground. This will only be successful if A has a faster pony than X and then he will have a tired pony for the rest of that chukka.

An experienced A will use the simple remedy of heading for the centre of the goal which his team is defending. Regardless of what happens to the ball A will stay on this course until he has passed X. Invariably the route taken by A will be considerably shorter than that of X whose shots will probably lack total accuracy. In fact X may also check slightly as he takes each shot. Therefore every stride taken by A will recover a bit of the ground originally lost. Even with a slower pony than that of X it is possible to recover ground especially if X's approach shot is inaccurate. However it is vital that A does not watch his opponent too closely until he has

gone past him. He should only see X out of the corner of his eye while his main concentration is on the direct route to goal. In this way any possibility of distraction which would interfere with the recovery of ground is avoided. Once A has clearly gone past X so that he is between X and the goal he can look around.

A only has to check a little before closing on X as he pursues the ball. Now the ground is recovered, the back door shut, X is marked and the pony of A will not have over exerted itself.

In exactly the same way you can recover ground as a defending No.3 against the opposing No.2, as the defending No.2 on an opposing No.3 and as a defending No.1 on an opposing No.4. Whether the opponents are in possession of the ball or not is irrelevant. All that matters is that they have taken an advantage from you through their good anticipation, or because of your mistake or from an unlucky bounce of the ball. Whatever the reason you have to cut a corner to regain the ground lost. Ball-chasing or watching will only ensure that your opponent will retain his advantage.

Once I played back in a low-goal tournament. In one of the matches the opposing No.1 was a celebrity who had very fast ponies. In one of the chukkas I was on a pony recently purchased from a well-known polo pony dealer. This gentleman, who is tall, was watching the match from the grandstand. I suddenly found that I had committed the worst mistake that a No.4 can make. I had arrived in our opponents' goalmouth and was standing in a bunch with the rest of my team. I had gone for a non-certainty and had left the back door completely open. One of the opponents had just hit a good angled back hand to the side line and the ball was about to reach the 60 yard line. The celebrity was in full gallop after the ball and about to strike it.

Luckily I remembered the tip once given to me by my father. This was how to recover ground. So I set off with my new pony straight down the centre of the ground from one goal in the direction of the other. The situation appeared hopeless until the celebrity hit one

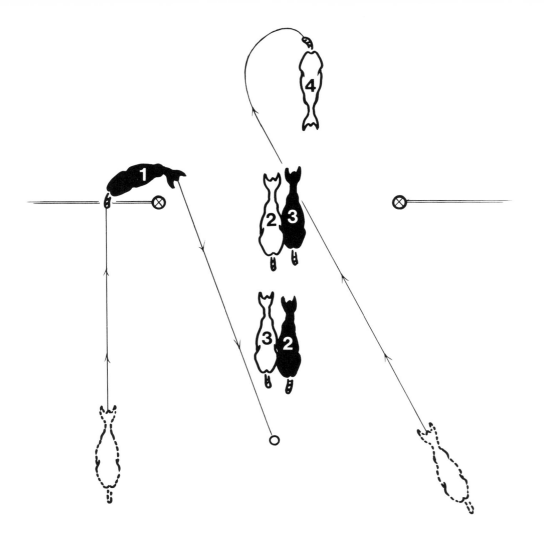

Goal post drill through which No. 1 may have a backhand shot at goal and otherwise will be perfectly placed for defence if required

shot more towards the side line than the goal. I was level with him as we crossed our defending 60 yard line. He was then halfway between me and the side line and had just struck a perfect approach shot to the 30 yard line. I was now closer to the goal and the ball than the celebrity and it was simple to win the ride-off and hit the backhand when we arrived at the 30 yard line.

The chukka then finished and we all cantered to the pony lines. Looking up I saw a tall man running towards me from the grandstand. ''You bastard I sold you that pony too cheap'' he yelled!

Going the shortest way to recover ground can make a pony look much faster than it is. Even an expert in the grandstand can easily be fooled in his judgement of pony speed. High-goal players control a game throughout with this technique and often finish a chukka with their ponies still fresh.

Bobby Moore, the English Captain in the 1960 and 1970 World Cup soccer tournaments, was not a very fast runner according to his team manager. Yet Pele the outstanding forward of all time said that Bobby Moore was the best defender he had ever played against. He would appear from nowhere and take the ball from an opponent about to shoot. On the soccer pitch Bobby Moore must have known how to recover ground.

GOAL POST DRILL

The rule of four players in four positions can be very difficult for a No. 1 to comply with when he arrives in front of the goal with the ball behind him. Maybe he has just been neutralised in a ride-off, or he has just missed the ball or he has galloped up the ground waiting for the pass that never arrived. Whatever the reason he knows that his team still has possession. What should he do now?

In low-goal polo a No. 1 in this situation will generally turn left or right and attempt, by the means of a full circle, to rejoin the game. While doing so the No. 1 is completely out of the game leaving his team with only three players. At the end of the circle he usually finds that he is muddling another team member and probably committing a foul by crossing the line of the ball. Alternatively he could make such a large circle that he comes in behind the rest of his team in the position of No. 4. In this case his team is down to three players for an even longer period of time. He will have crossed the barrier upsetting the tactical balance of his team for attack and defence.

Other players in this position are apt to loose their heads and continue straight through the goal which is the worst action a No. 1 could take. Why? Because an accurate shot at goal from his team may be deflected by his pony and made to miss the goal.

A high handicap No. 1 can adjust with such agility that he does not have this problem. His extra sense of anticipation will keep him in the play. But the low handicap player needs a drill always in the back of his mind, which he can use in this difficult situation. Therefore the No. 1 should aim his pony to pass outside the nearest goal post. Normally this will be the left hand post because the No. 1 will probably have been directing his pony to this post all the way up the ground. Why? So that he can link to goal by receiving any pass that may arrive on his offside. Also by doing this his pony will not impede or deflect any accurate shot that is struck from behind him. If, however, the goal is attacked from or via the right hand side line the No. 1 may find that he is on the wrong side of the goal and should go for the right hand goal post.

Once the No. 1 has arrived at and outside one of the goal posts he must halt. He should stop exactly at the goal post either through perfect pony control or by going on past the post and then returning to it after a sharp turn. From this position he is now prepared for whatever might take place. How many different situations could arise? Three. His team could score and he would not interfere; the ball could arrive in front of and close to the goal after players from both teams have galloped over it — in which case No. 1 can pass through the goal and score with an offside backhand; or, thirdly, an opponent may hit a backhand sending his team from defence into attack. No.1 is perfectly placed to follow the new main road (line of the ball) and early close the opposing No.4 or whoever is their last player. If another attack is set up by his own team the No.1 is placed to early turn and link to goal once more.

This drill can be done by the two players in front of the barrier, if the No.3 and No.4 are maintaining possession and are clearly not committing themselves. In this case neither of them will need covering by the No.2. They should each go for a different goal post. The one who arrives first must be the player to return through the goal posts if there is a chance to score with a backhand. However if the other player although arriving second obviously has the line of the ball he should go through the goal to make the backhander.

When coming through the goal to score it is important to hit to the offside. Why? Because a nearside backhand could cause a foul through meeting an opponent on the wrong side. To ensure that no foul occurs when coming through the goal to make the offside backhand, a little adjustment to be exactly on the line may be necessary.

A low-goal team which had received a little coaching from me before a specific tournament sent me the following telegram "winning goal scored by goal post drill".

One word of warning. Before going for the goal post to do this drill you must ensure that you are in attack and not defence! I was lucky enough once to play No.2 in a fourteen goal team which entered one of the most important English medium-goal tournaments. Behind me in our team was the incredibly long hitting Hector Barantes (7) and against us the formidable and consistent striker of length Paul Withers (7). At times the game appeared to me to be so fast that all sense of position became rather blurred. At one moment I was flying down the ground at an unbelieveable speed when the computer in my head told me "goal post drill". As I rounded the goal post I found myself in a head on collision with Hector Barantes and the opposing No.1. My computer had let me down, we were in defence not attack and Hector was about to save off our goal line. I will never forget the roar of agonised disbelief from Hector, a great character and a fabulous team player. I felt that he would never forgive me especially when at the end of the match we only lost by half a goal.

Chapter 13

POLO RIDING "D"

RIDING IN FOURS

In Chapter 10 we looked at how you can ride in pairs round the school. We saw that you could conform to your pair and to the remainder of the ride. This required you to become completely outside your pony. To extend this exercise further and make you look at even more people at the same time the next progression is to ride in fours.

Once again one person is the leader and he controls all the movements in the school by verbal commands or hand signals. Let us presume that you are riding in pairs around the school and the leading pair on each side is approaching one of the ends. The leader gives the command "in fours down the line". As they reach that end of the school the pairs merge into fours and proceed down the line. At the other end of the line the first four turns left, the second four turns right, and so on.

Now each four must stay together and at the same time remain opposite the four on the other side. This necessitates a continual adjustment being made by all the eight riders. Each four must be pivoted by the inside man who is trying to stay opposite the other four yet never permitting the three with him to be left behind. He should take a route round the school that allows his outside man to use the full width of the school without being crushed. Therefore he will have to change pace continuously and be prepared almost to halt at times. This involves looking at the other four and his own outside man throughout by letting his eyes swing from left to right. If, despite all the above, his four fail to keep up with the opposite four the inside man must cut the next corner. If he sees that his four is ahead of the opposite four he should gently push his outside man right into the next corner.

The outside man for most of the time should use the full width of the school by steering his pony along the perimeter. If he places himself fractionally ahead of the other three he can stay in the correct position and accelerate effortlessly at each corner. He has the furthest to go and therefore must be travelling that little bit faster than the others. However he only has to look in one direction to see and conform to his inside man and the opposite four at the same time. If his four fall behind despite his acceleration he must leave the perimeter and cut a corner. If his four are too far ahead he should go right into a corner to slow them up.

The two men in the middle simply have to stay between their inside and outside men. For some this is not so simple because they continuously look at their pony. What happens then? They are not "outside their pony" and therefore totally unable to adjust to the others. The secret to avoid being squeezed out of line is to place yourself between the inside and outside men by swinging your eyes left and right without ever seeing your pony. Out of the corner of your eye you should see the opposite four, although your inside man is mainly responsible for the adjustments in relation to them.

As before, at the end of the school the fours will pass right hand to right hand. That is to say those going clockwise are always on the outside by the perimeter. Therefore, the inside man of the inside four needs to steer a clever and exact route so that his outside man passes very close to the opposing inside man. Then the next corner must be rounded slowly to allow the other four to remain opposite. The outside man of the outside four requires even more acceleration than usual for that next corner.

When both fours are settled together and remaining constantly opposite each other the leader can command or signal "join the line". The inside men slow up more than ever to try to make their outside men come together comfortably on the line. The outside men should only look at each other accelerating to join that line as a pair. The middle men as ever look left and right to stay in the four. Hopefully you are now eight going down the

Riding in fours without looking around

line abreast until the leader gives "away". The inside man may almost have to stop to bring his four round him and place the outside man out on the perimeter once more.

Next the leader gives "cross the school and change the rein". Immediately the roles are reversed for the inside and outside men. The new inside men need perfect pony control, without seeing their ponies, to change from accelerating to slowing up. Thus they pivot their four while conforming to the opposite four. All eight riders will probably need to make hasty adjustments to stay in position. If they remain "outside the ponies" throughout it will be done smoothly and effortlessly allowing the leader to order "join the line" soon afterwards. But if anyone looks at their ponies there will be chaos and the leader will have to wait for two or three rounds of the school or even call a halt in order to reassemble before he can proceed with the next "join the line".

It is amazing how easily the ponies will conform to "riding in fours" if the riders stay outside their ponies and make the correct adjustments by looking in the required directions. Everyone that I have trained has found that riding in fours is the greatest fun and most exhilarating. If you can stay in a four without making a mistake during a series of "join the line and cross the school to change the rein" you will then find pair riding very much easier. From this "riding-off" and marking a good player will become simpler.

A suggested programme for a leader when the riders are in fours on the first occasion is as follows:-

At the walk down the middle in fours. At

the end of the line first four left second four right. Join the line, away, cross the school change the rein, join the line, away, cross the school change the rein. Repeat at the trot; repeat at the canter. If anything goes wrong do the last movement again. If there is a muddle go back to the walk. If there is chaos call a halt and possibly change one or two positions so that you have a different inside or outside man in one of the fours.

Obviously it is possible to be three on each side of the school, or to work with three on one side and four on the other. If your numbers are only six or seven after operating in pairs the leader could bring you all to the line, halt and then reorganise. With only one middle man three riders will still have considerable adjustments to make although control will be easier than with four.

Diagonal across the school

This is another way of crossing the school. When you are in single file in two rides on opposite sides of the school you can cross diagonally from one corner to another. The leader gives the command or signal. The simplest task falls to 1. On arrival at the next corner he goes across the school diagonally to the opposite corner where he changes rein. From his corner 2 will start and then aim to pass just behind the tail of 1's pony before proceeding on the other diagonal. Then 3 should aim for the tail of 2 and 4 for the tail of 3 and so on. All change the rein in the corner at the end of the diagonal.

The secret for achieving a smooth movement is that each rider should aim at the relevant tail from the moment he leaves the

corner. He cannot follow the diagonal and hope for the best. Therefore you start in a similar direction as for a direct crossing of the school allowing the head of your pony to point at the man who is leaving the opposite corner. There is, then, a continual adjustment required to keep the head of your pony constantly aimed at his tail. This will automatically draw you to the centre of the school where you will pass behind the other pony.

After an outwards turn each side of the school would be led by the highest number. For example, if there are eight riders, 8 and 7 will be leading. To make the diagonal crossing 8 will go first followed by 7, 6 and so on.

The exercise must be done slowly and repeated until it is clear that all understand and can execute the method of continual adjustment to the tail of the pony crossing in front. If one rider proceeds straight to the centre every time and waits there for a pony to cross in front, the ride should be halted. This individual should then practice with one partner until he achieves the correct method. Then the leader is safe to allow the diagonal to be done at speed.

Not only is this further training for good pony control and for making precise adjustments, but it can teach you a useful trick. The art of hooking sticks when moving at right angles to your opponent without intimidating or fouling him. This can only be done if the opponent is not being followed by another of his team. It is especially useful when an adversary on your nearside has placed himself to hit the ball in such a way that to ride him off is impossible.

Chapter 14

STRIKING "D"

NEARSIDE FOREHAND CUT

This is possibly the hardest shot of all. It is difficult to achieve the required length and accuracy with the limited swing. Yet if the five basic rules of striking are applied a vital goal might be scored with this shot. If the goal is to your left, one opponent is pushing against you on your right and another is behind you unmarked, you will have to attempt it.

The pony is placed so that the ball can be hit late and far out. Depending on various factors the ball should be somewhere between seven and eight o'clock in relation to the pony when struck.

The stick and hand position is the same as for the near side forehand straight shot and the offside backhand. Which is? Vertical with the right hand at the left shirt pocket.

The shoulders swivel as far to the left as possible so that the ball can be seen under the right shoulder. The right hand touches the point of the left shoulder. The fork position on the saddle turns left. The right heel is up in the air stretching the iron against the leather for support unless you are in a ride-off.

Your head goes down to focus on the sweet spot between four and five o'clock on the ball. The back of the right hand guides the stick to the sweet spot from your left shoulder giving you the maximum available swing.

The follow through is carried on by the back of the hand to a point between ten and eleven o'clock in relation to the pony. The fork position must remain to the left to allow the swing and follow through to be in a straight line.

You should not waste too much time in practising the shot. It could upset the pony and yourself. Other shots are more important. Use the wooden horse to show yourself that the shot is possible and occasionally slip one into your stick and ball programme.

NEARSIDE FOREHAND UNDER THE NECK

This should be much easier than the cut shot as there is a longer swing and your weight remains above the pony. Throughout, the basic rules apply as follows:-

Place the pony to hit the ball early. In relation to the pony the ball should be between ten and eleven o'clock.

The hand and stick position is again at the left shirt pocket.

The shoulders swing to the left to bring the right shoulder to point at the ball. As this is a relatively small turn of the shoulders compared with the cut shot there is the danger you may only do the movement in a half-hearted manner. In fact the right leg and whole fork should pivot fully to the left to ensure that excessive arm strength is not applied. The right hand touches the point of the left shoulder before the back of the hand starts the swing.

Your head goes down to focus on the sweet spot between seven and eight o'clock on the ball. From the left shoulder the back of the hand moves to the sweet spot taking full advantage of such a long swing.

The follow through under the neck goes to the target which should be between one and two o'clock in relation to the pony. The back of the hand must exert complete control to conform to your mental picture of where the target is. It is so easy to over or under pull and if you are shooting at goal it will be a very narrow one. Why? Because from the side the width of the goal is reduced.

Beware not to over use this shot if you are unattended by an opponent. A small adjustment in the approach to the ball can convert the shot into an offside cut giving you less possibility of inaccuracy.

NEARSIDE BACKHAND ROUND THE TAIL

Many people are frightened to make this shot and others never even attempt it. The ability to hit it will add much to the flexibility of team tactics and sometimes enable an extra goal to be scored.

If a precise application of the five rules is used, after a little practice, confidence will increase considerably. Placing the pony to the ball accurately is vital before the shot can be attempted. Otherwise you will hit the legs of the pony or give the ball to an opponent waiting behind you. The ball should be between seven and eight o'clock in relation to the pony. The head of the pony can be inclined a little to the left to reduce the angle to be hit through round the tail. However, if there is an opponent behind you care must be taken not to cross the line during or after the shot.

The hand and stick position is in front and inside the right shoulder.

The left shoulder should initially move to the right and under your chin. Then the whole body turns left and the left shoulder points at the ball. This movement is completed and secured by the fork turning on the saddle. The heel of the right leg points upwards and at right angles to the pony.

The sweet spot is between ten and eleven o'clock on the ball. Minimum force is needed to reach it. The length of the swing will provide sufficient strength.

The follow through goes to five o'clock in relation to the pony while your fork position on the saddle remains still and secure.

EXERCISES
Interchange A

A and B work together. They start with the ball placed between them and in the middle of the ground. They are both facing the ball and move at the same time towards it. A places his pony to hit a backhand out to his right. B moves to his left to go past the ball and past A as, or even slightly before, the backhand is hit. A backhands to his right and to B who joins the line before making a quiet forehand. A turns to follow B.

A: "Place the pony, sweet spot, adjust to follow B."

B: "Pass by A, look behind me at A, join the line, place the pony, sweet spot."

Next B goes past the ball again before turning to his left. A backhands to his left and to B who joins the line before making a quiet forehand.

B: "Pass over the ball, look behind me at A, turn, join the line, sweet spot."

A: "Place the pony, sweet spot, adjust to follow B."

Next B repeats the last movement except that he turns to the right. A backhands to his right and to B who, if the situation allows shoots at goal. Commentary is as before. The exercise now restarts with B taking the backhands and A forehands.

Interchange B

A and B start together at one end of the ground behind the back line, with the ball placed for a hit-in. A hits the ball towards the 60 yard line and in the direction of the left hand far corner before following it to make a forehand cut shot aimed at the far goal. Initially B follows A until reaching the 30 yard line. There he accelerates in the direction of the far goal so as to go past A and receive the ball from his forehand cut shot.

A: "Head down, sweet spot, follow ball, look behind me to see B, approach for cut shot, head down, sweet spot."

B: "Adjust to A, head for goal, look behind me, join the line."

Now B hits the ball quietly towards the far right hand corner and follows it to make a forehand under the neck shot in the direction of goal. A for a moment follows B towards the far right corner and then accelerates in the direction of goal. He goes past B placing himself to receive the ball from the forehand under the neck shot.

B: "Look at right hand corner, head down, sweet spot, follow the ball, look behind me to see A, approach for under the neck shot, head down, sweet spot."

A: "Adjust behind B, head for goal, look behind me, join the line."

The above is repeated until either A or B arrive with the ball at the far 30 yard line and are in a position to shoot at goal. The exercise then restarts with B taking the forehand cut shots and A the forehand under the neck shots. Close co-operation is required between A and

Nearside forehand cut

(Opposite page) *Stick and hand position*
(Left) *Shoulder*
(Below) *Sweet spot*

Nearside forehand under the neck

Stick and hand position Shoulder

Sweet spot

Stick and hand position

earside backhand round the tail

oulder   *Sweet spot*

B. After cutting or pulling the ball they must, if necessary, slow down sufficiently or even stop to allow their partner room and time to proceed.

Recovering ground

This could be done by two or three people. However with three you can make the exercise continuous which is more beneficial. Therefore it will be explained as carried out by *A*, *B* and *C*.

A starts from the left hand side line at the 60 yard line. *B* comes through the near goal with *C* moving parallel to him about thirty yards to his right. *A* heads for the far goal hitting the ball quietly. *B* goes straight down the middle of the ground on a line between the two goals recovering ground from *A*. *C* remains to the right and parallel with *B*.

A: "Look at the goal, approach the ball, head down, sweet spot." This is then repeated for each shot.

B: "Look at the goal, keep going straight for the goal, only see *A* out of the corner of the eye."

C: "Conform to *B*, adjust."

Now *A* and *B* engage in a ride-off. *A* allows *B* to win and to hit a backhand to his right and out towards the right hand side line. *C* early turns and joins the line of the ball, collects the ball at or near the side line and heads for the near goal. *A* adjusts to be exactly in the centre of the ground, turns around and goes straight for the near goal recovering ground from *C*. *B* turns left and then adjusts to be thirty yards to the right of and parallel with *A*.

C: "Adjust to *B*, turn, join the line, look at the goal, approach the goal, head down, sweet spot."

A: "Let *B* win ride-off, look behind me, adjust, turn, look at goal, keep straight for goal, only observe *C* out of the corner of the eye."

B: "Look at *A*, early close to *A*, place pony for backhand, sweet spot, look behind me, turn left, conform to *A*, keep to his right."

Next *C* and *A* engage in a ride-off. *C* allows *A* to win and hit a backhand to his right and out to the side line from which he originally started. *B* early turns, joins the line with the ball, collects the ball at or near the side line and heads for the far goal. *C* adjusts to be exactly in the centre of the ground, turns around and goes straight for the far goal. *A* turns left and then adjusts to be thirty yards to the right of and parallel with *C*.

B: "Adjust to *A*, turn, join the line, look at the goal, approach goal, head down, sweet spot."

C: "Let *A* win ride-off, look behind me, adjust, turn, look at goal, keep straight for goal, only see *B* out of corner of the eye."

A: "Look at *C*, early close to *C*, place pony for backhand, sweet spot, look behind me, turn left, conform to *C* and keep to his right."

After *C* has recovered ground, ridden off *B* and backhanded to *A* the three will be once again positioned with *A* on the left, *B* in the centre and *C* to his right.

Chapter 15

TACTICS "E"

HOW TO BEAT A BETTER TEAM

Let us imagine that you are in a good team which obeys the rules for the four positions, the set pieces and interchanges. But one day your team is confronted by a better team. In fact your opponents are quicker and in general hit the ball further than your team. Other than hoping for luck to favour you, how can the match be won?

You have to remove from your opponents the main advantage which they hold over you. They are quicker than you and therefore you must slow down the game. How? There are three simple tactics that can be employed.

All backhands to the side lines

Unless you have crossed your opponents 60 yard line in attack, nearly all backhands from your No.3 and No.4 should be angled acutely towards the side lines. This does not mean that you are trying to hit the ball out, but that you are forcing your opponents away from the centre of the ground. Inevitably this will slow them up as they will be unable to use the quickest route to goal. Instead they will be continually moving laterally and away from your goal. Their forehands will have to be angled after which there will be a delay as they rejoin the line of the ball. Your forwards should always turn out, and not in, towards the centre thus making anticipation that much easier.

Early close more persistently

Whenever an opponent is near you, close to him and slow him down. Even when the ball is in front of you with the ride-off won, instead of accelerating to keep control of your opponent, push him further to the side and slow down. Not only will this blunt the speed of the opposition but it will give your team more time to adjust into the next positions.

A cool No.3 can take this tactic to an extreme by dribbling a short way towards his own goal before angling the backhand to the side. However this should only be done because he sees that there is no one to pass to at that moment or that a team member needs more time to adjust into the best position to receive the ball.

The opposing No.3 and No.4 should be ridden-off for much of the game and not only when the ball is near them. Besides slowing up their mobility around the ground it will also impede and reduce their anticipation.

Change the direction of play

When in attack somewhere on the left hand side of the ground, a pass will normally be sent in the direction of goal from *A* to *B*. The forehand by *A* will ideally be placed to arrive on the right hand side of *B*. However, against a strong opposition, nine times out of ten, this will simply give possession to your opponents. *X*, who is marking *B*, will win the ensuing ride-off and hit a backhand. Why? Because *X* will be correctly positioned just behind *B* expecting this forehand from *A* and ready to early close.

Instead *A* could possibly make a different approach to the ball placing his pony to hit a backhand. This shot could be angled to arrive further to the right of *B* than normal. If *B* knows that this will happen and *X* does not, the element of surprise will assist *B*. Because of this change in the direction of play *X* will have less time and further to move before he can close for the ride off. Therefore *B* should use this advantage to make the next shot and maintain possession for his team.

Naturally in this situation *A* must first look around to ensure that his approach to the ball will not cause a foul. An opponent close by could join the line in the hope that *A* will cross him.

During an attack on the right hand side of the ground a similar change of direction can be made by *A*. This time his backhand should be angled to arrive on the left side of *B* instead of his right. It is vital that *B* is prepared for this, whereas *X* is not, so that the maximum advantage can be gained.

Tactics "E"

Slowing up the game by changing the direction of play

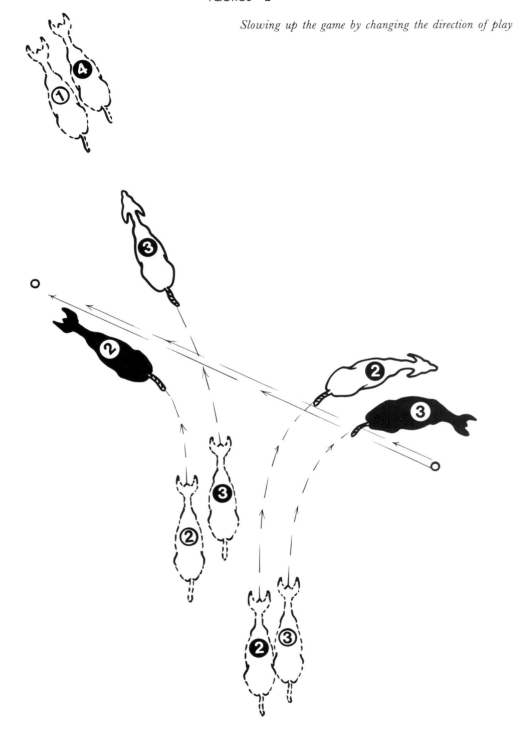

Besides producing an unexpected change in direction this tactic of the angled backhand instead of a forehand will also slow up the game. The shot from *A* will be made a second later than anticipated and the fastest route to goal will be circumvented. If you add to this the defensive backhands to the side line and the persistent early closing, the opponents will seldom be able to play at their top speed.

I have been both the victim and the perpetrator of these tactics. In many sports, especially soccer and tennis, the same method is often used by the under-dog who has made a specific plan before the game. Yet, in low-goal polo the majority of players and teams go on to the ground only thinking about ball-chasing. If your opponent can chase the ball faster than you then a heavy defeat is inevitable. The euphoria that can be felt when victory is achieved against known better opponents is wonderful. Even if you lose, but make the game into a close contest, enormous satisfaction is achieved.

OPPOSING PENALTIES

It is surprising how many times a penalty shot fails to score. Furthermore the team opposing a penalty can often change the situation to their own advantage and maybe even score a gaol at the other end of the ground. For this to happen more than good luck is needed. It occurs because the opposition is well organised. Besides applying extra pressure on the penalty striker they are sometimes capable of saving a well struck shot.

Hit from the centre or spot

The team could use a modification of the box formation and meeting tactics already described for facing the hit-in. Instead of the angled line across the ground made by No.2 and No.3 and No.4 a shallow half circle — in the order No.2, No.4 and No.3 — might cover all eventualities. Thus, No.4 is still the last man but in the centre of the team line up. However the opponents must be carefully watched so that they can all be individually marked if necessary. They may use an unconventional tactic which will have to be

adjusted to. The No.1 acts exactly as when facing the hit-in and should do his utmost to prevent the hitter from tapping the ball more than once.

60 yard penalty

The only rule that applies to the team defending against the 60 yard penalty is that all their players must be behind the 30 yard line.

In planning the positions of the players and the various actions which they should take there are two main considerations. Firstly, how to prevent the ball from going through the goal and, secondly, to employ a plan which ensures that a further foul is not committed bringing about the stiffer penalty of a 30 yard penalty.

It is sad for a team to make a good save only to find that the opponents then have a second and easier chance to score. It is ridiculous if the penalty hitter is fouled after making a weak or inaccurate shot. Yet it is surprising how many times the second consideration is unheeded in a polo match and an unnecessary goal is thereby given away.

But if No.1 and No.2 stand together, nose to tail, sideways to the hitter with the No.1 stick side exposed to the ball all eventualities can be covered. How many are there? There are seven as follows:- the hitter may (i) mis-hit the ball; (ii) tap it or (iii) hit inaccurately. Alternatively the ball could hit one of the two ponies or players and be deflected (iv); to the left (v); to the right or (vi) drop dead on the stick side of the No.1; the ball may come hard and straight passing over or under the two ponies (vii).

For the first three eventualities No.1 can compete with the penalty hitter for the next shot. If the fourth happens the ball will land in front of No.1. Therefore, he will now be on the new "line" and by moving to hit the ball he will cease to stand on the old line. However No.2 must also move forward immediately in the opposite direction in order that the old line is cleared for the penalty hitter to come at speed.

When the fifth occurs the ball will land in

front of No.2. This will give him the new line and allow him to leave the old one as he advances to strike the ball. Now No.1 should quickly move in the opposite direction to clear the old line.

These two eventualities aptly bring out an example of an "old" and "new" line situation which need not be confusing once explained. On many occasions during polo games there is a brief moment after a new line is established when the old line maintains priority. This happens because a player has committed himself at speed on the old line and initially is unable to stop.

The sixth possibility demonstrates how the old and new line can be one and the same. Therefore if either No.1 or No.2 remain stationary they will be standing at right angles to the penalty hitter who has the line. No.2 can only move forward and out of the way. No.1, however, is in a position to hit the ball and possibly threaten the goal at the far end. But if before moving he hits the ball which is lying under him the whistle will blow for a cross. So how can he avoid fouling? He must first move his pony to be on the opposite side of the line and facing the penalty hitter. Then No.1 can wait a second to give the penalty hitter the illusion that the ball can be hit again. After this No.1 should tap the ball under his pony's neck towards the left hand side line and follow it. In this way he will have made and joined a new line without ever obstructing the old one. However, great care must be taken not to intimidate the penalty hitter who, once committed, will have to continue forward leaving the back door wide open.

The seventh eventuality will remove all responsibility from No.1 and No.2 as the ball speeds towards the goal mouth. Here No.3 and No.4 should be positioned to defend against the ball in the air or on the ground. To do this it will help if both of them cover half of the goal area against the former and a whole goal area against the latter. Is this possible? Yes, if No.3 stands on the line with No.4 exactly half a length behind him. Then, for the lofted ball, No.4 moves forward alongside

No.3 and with their polo sticks raised each one tries to stop the ball in the air. But, for the ball on the ground, No.3 goes forward to meet it a few yards in front of the goal line while No.4 stays behind to attempt a stop on the goal line. Thus, both have a chance to save and on the goal line No.4 will meet the ball at its lowest velocity.

30 yard and 40 yard penalty

For both these penalties the rules are the same. All must be behind the back line until the ball is struck. No one can stand between the goal posts or come through them after the ball is hit. If any player crosses the back line early and a goal is missed the penalty can be retaken. However, if the ball that was *en route* to go through the goal is stopped by a player who moved early it will be counted as a goal.

There is a job for each player. These are not related to their positions in the team but to individual and pony abilities. Therefore we will call the players A, B, C, D. Basically two of them are there to attempt a save and the other two positions so as to call out if the ball is missing the goal. There are three likely occurrences from the 30 yard or 40 yard penalty: (i) a well hit accurate shot; (ii) a hard hit inaccurate shot; (iii) a tap or mis-hit.

A and B stand one either side of the goal. For the second occurrence they are ready to call out "missing". For the first or third occurrence they stay and keep quiet. C can start from left or right hand sides of the goal. Normally the right hand side is used in order to put the ball on his stick side. The presumption is that the penalty striker feeling and seeing his shot going fast towards the goal will stop to admire the result. Therefore, no one will be following the line of the ball which can be crossed safely at right angles by C without committing a foul. Hence C should be cantering along and behind the back line, ready to cross it as the ball is struck. Thus it is a possibility that he will arrive in front and between the goal posts at the same time as the ball. C now has a reasonable chance to deflect the ball away from the goal with either his polo stick or the pony. If the second occurrence happens C, hearing the call of ''missing'' stops, turns and adjusts in order to allow the ball to cross the back line unimpeded. For the third occurrence C stops or turns to avoid crossing the penalty striker who will be following the ball. In this case D, who is positioned just outside the left hand goal post, has the task to save, meet the ball or dispossess the penalty striker. He must first adjust laterally to be exactly on the line and in order not to intimidate the penalty striker.

There is a considerable danger that C and D will muddle one another and even have a collision. The onus is on D to watch C closely at the same time as he observes the penalty striker and not to move until it is clearly safe to do so. I have often carried out the task of C and have experienced both the elation of saving a certain goal and the agony of ending up as a battered heap on the ground. As an umpire I have frequently incurred the wrath of a player who in the role of C has fouled the penalty striker. He had failed to adjust to events yet felt badly wronged by my decision! In fact such a foul could easily be punished with Penalty 1. This is given for a dangerous foul which is committed deliberately to save a goal. Without changing ends a goal is awarded and a throw-in takes place in front of the goal mouth ten yards from the centre of the goal.

Chapter 16

POLO RIDING "E"

LOOK AT ME AND TURN

This is a movement which can teach you how to turn a pony at speed when something unexpected takes place in a game. The ball may have hit a pony or another player may have changed the direction of play with a completely unanticipated shot.

If you are in the school with other riders the procedure is as follows. All except one stand together on the line in the centre of the school. This one rider, X, starts from the end of the line. He goes as fast as possible in the direction of the left hand far corner. His eyes should be firmly fixed on that corner. After X has passed the centre the instructor calls out "look at me". X obeys but continues in the direction of the corner at the same speed. When X and his pony have taken two more strides the leader says "turn". Without taking his eyes away from the instructor, even for a split second, X turns his pony 180 degrees to the right. He then looks at, and proceeds towards, the corner which is now to his right. Once again the leader calls "look at me" and after two strides "turn". X obeys and turns to the left.

If done correctly the well-trained pony will turn sharply under the rider on the spot. Many people find it difficult not to look forward or down during the turn. This will prevent the pony making a quick turn. Why? Because the rider's weight will momentarily swing against the direction of the turn.

Each rider should repeat this exercise several times until he has done it correctly. It is very similar to the outwards turn but here you have the extra demand on you in that the remainder of the riders will see if you look away.

If you are not with other riders you can ask another person on foot to call out the commands. Otherwise you could use a prominent object like a tree and call out the commands yourself. "Look at the tree" pause "turn".

In a game you can apply this exercise by deliberately looking at another player while turning. Alternatively a goal post or object like a car on the side line could be used as a reference point.

A high-goal player frequently makes sharp turns during a polo match without any thought of how to do it. Why? Because he is 100% outside his pony and automatically does the motions of this exercise.

RIDING IN EIGHTS

If you can ride around and across the school in fours, there will be little difficulty if the numbers are increased. The higher the number the more precise everyone will have to be with their adjustments to each other. This is the best possible way to improve pony control.

The exercises when riding in fours have been explained. Let us imagine that the two groups of four are opposite each other and approaching one end of the school.

The leader gives the command to go down the line as an eight. The two outside men join together on the line. The two inside men slow down to allow the remainder to make a line abreast between them. All move down the line, looking left and right to keep together. At the end of the line the leader instructs the eight to turn left or right.

The eight is controlled by the left hand and the right hand men. One is moving along the school perimeter often increasing speed to keep the eight abreast. The other, the inside man, places himself on a course which allows seven ponies to fit comfortably between his pony and the school perimeter. He is continually slowing down to ensure that he does not go in front of the outside man. The remaining six riders look left and right throughout the movements to stay correctly line abreast. If any one looks at his pony, or to his front, for more than that fleeting moment between looking left and right, the formation will go out of control. You must place yourself in the line abreast and then bring your pony with you adjusting to the other seven continuously.

If the eight are moving around the school smoothly the leader can instruct them to join the line. The outside man has to accelerate rapidly to reach the line. Then he places himself parallel to it so that the middle two, 4 and 5, are actually on the line. The inside man should slow down more than ever to allow the other seven to pivot around him to the line. If necessary he must even stop for a second to avoid leaving anyone behind. The remaining six conform and adjust to each other to stay in formation as the eight proceeds along the line. The command "away" follows almost immediately and the whole procedure is repeated until the outside man is on the perimeter again. Hence the inside man has allowed the other seven to complete a circle around him.

After this the eight continue around the school as before until the leader gives the order "cross the school and change the rein". The inside and outside men exchange roles immediately the eight have crossed the centre line. The sudden change from accelerating to slowing down or vice versa will need excellent control. This can only be achieved by watching and conforming to the other seven ponies and riders throughout.

A series of joining the line and crossing the school to change the rein can be ordered by the instructor. This should be built up from the walk to the trot and then to the canter. Everyone will be tested to the full in their ability to adjust to others. At the walk the outside riders will at times need to trot. It follows that they may have to canter when the others trot and gallop to conform to the inside man at the canter. If the formation is broken

and a rider is left behind, the only solution is a halt or to order the eight back to a walk.

Obviously the same movements can be done by six or seven riders. After a few days of enjoying the exercises in the riding school a group of riders should be able to work through the various movements singly, in pairs, in fours and finally in eights. The four principles of polo riding, outside your pony, minimum hands, look and go and strong legs will of necessity have been applied. If, for a few minutes each day, the riders are without stirrups the legs can be further strengthened. The fifth rule, weight on the front of the saddle can be achieved by the riders continually checking their position in the saddle and by frequent reminders from the instructor.

Any pony that will do all these exercises in the riding school without resisting the wishes of its rider, can surely respond to any requirements of a player in a polo match. If you have more than one pony it would be advisable to ride a different one each day in the school. Every pony can benefit from taking part. Both rider and pony will learn how to combine together to answer the demands of a fast game. Everyone should experiment to find the method that is most acceptable to each pony for all the movements. For example, some ponies will react better when controlled by two hands instead of one. Many of the best players often use two hands when a very accurate adjustment is necessary. Perhaps you can be more gentle with two hands? In a game, when carrying a polo stick, the fingers of the right hand can be placed in front of the left hand to hold the reins.

Chapter 17

STRIKING "E"

HITTING THE BALL HARDER

In the previous chapters on striking we have discussed ten shots. Economy was emphasised so that the ball is struck quietly and strength of the arm is seldom used. However, once you have learnt to hit with the correct technique and have achieved consistent accuracy the time will come to increase the length of shot.

Arm strength is still not to be employed and it is important not to upset your basic timing. Therefore, how do you satisfy the three requirements of length, no strength and timing? You should experiment how to make the stick head travel faster through the air during the execution of each shot. There are different ways of doing this and you must find the system that suits you. For each shot two methods will now be looked at. An economic method first and then a more extravagant way of speeding up the stick head. Ideally, you should start with the economic method and later in your polo career progress to a mixture of the economic and the extravagant way.

Offside forehand — economic

Stick and hand position is as before. When "drawing the bow" the stick head is deliberately left above the head while the right hand moves back. Then as the right hand comes forward again the stick head will have to catch up the cane before the sweet spot is struck.

Offside forehand — extravagant

The stick is swung fully around one or more times before the right hand moves back to draw the bow. Beware of using arm strength, standing in the stirrups and hitting late. To prevent these happening the preparatory swing should be started early during the approach to the ball. Then the left shoulder must be pointed at the ball to make the fork turn to the right and remain on the saddle.

The way some players drop the stick head forward and down is completely wrong. To lift the stick up again is laborious and will slow up your swing. Hence it is difficult to hit early. Many low-goal players in England and Germany have this habit. It may work well during stick and ball but, when they play in a fast game, they all hit late.

Offside backhand — economic

The stick and hand position is normal. When the right hand moves to touch the left shoulder the stick head is allowed to drop sideways towards your head. The cane may be placed in front or behind your head, whichever is preferred. With the right shoulder pointing at the ball the right hand makes exactly the same swing and follow through as before. But the stick head will have to travel further and faster to arrive on time at the sweet spot.

Offside backhand — extravagant

The stick position is changed so as to point at the ground close to the right foot. The right hand starts by the girth and moves towards the left shoulder as the right shoulder points at the ball. From there the right hand seeks out the sweet spot.

Nearside forehand — economic

Stick and hand position is normal. As the right hand touches the left shoulder the stick head is allowed to fall forward. The right shoulder points at the ball and the usual swing hurries the stick head to strike the sweet spot.

Nearside forehand — extravagant

The stick position is in front of the left foot with the right hand by the left knee. The right hand lifts to the left shoulder as the right shoulder points at the ball. The total swing is greatly increased provided that it starts early enough.

Nearside backhand — economic

From the normal stick and hand position move the right hand out to the right and upwards. When the right arm is fully stretched, point the left shoulder at the ball and seek out the sweet spot.

Nearside backhand — extravagant

The stick position is in front of the left foot. The right hand makes a complete clockwise circle which passes close to your head before finding the sweet spot.

Until you can afford to be extravagant and make the shots without hurry it is better to retain the principle of economy. This will ensure that you hit the ball early and accurately.

HOOKING STICKS

Hooking sticks is an important part of good marking. However competent you are at "early closing" there will be occasions when you are too late to effect a ride-off. Instead there may well be a possibility of hooking the stick. Many players often miss this opportunity in the mistaken belief that they are too far away. If you put two polo sticks on the ground, end to end, you will see from how far away it is possible to hook an opponent. Of course this only applies if an opponent fully extends his arm to make an offside forehand shot.

Rules

The rules for hooking forbid you to hook across an opponent's pony. The ball must be between you and his pony. He must be making a shot when you hit his stick. You may not hook when his stick is above the shoulder. You are permitted to hit his stick firmly but not extremely hard.

Execution

The secret of hooking is not to look at the ball but to fix your eyes on the correct part of the opponent's stick. On the cane about two inches above the stick head is the best place. This becomes the sweet spot which should be focused upon before starting the hooking movement.

It is possible to hook forehands and backhands on the offside and on the nearside. The majority occur on the offside forehand and this is the hook which will now be explained.

Method

To make a successful hook your own polo stick is held so that the heel of the stick head is pointing upwards. To allow room for error you aim with the same part of the cane as that with which you were about to hook on your opponent's stick. How much inaccuracy does this permit? About four inches.

You can either swing the stick under your pony's neck or start from the nearside. The latter is used the most. The swing is upwards which should make contact against the other stick coming downwards. Between five and four o'clock in relation to your opponent's pony is the best place to make the hook. In fact well before the stick passes the right leg of your opponent.

Do not hang out your stick! Your opponent will probably hit through it and still strike the ball. A firm movement of your stick is required to stop the considerable velocity of his stick.

EXERCISES

Linking with two polo balls

This is the same as before except that two polo balls are used. As A is hitting a forehand pass to B with ball X, B is making a quiet approach shot with ball Y. In this way ball X should overtake ball Y. B then joins the line of ball X and makes another quiet approach shot. Meanwhile, A hits a forehand pass to B, this time with ball Y.

Thus A and B can bring the two polo balls the length of the ground in an attempt to score with both. If there is a mis-hit, causing one of the balls to be left behind before they reach the far 30 yard line, A and B should circle. Then they can restart with a ball each from that part of the ground where the balls are lying. If this happens after they have passed the 30 yard line, one or both of them can do "the goal post drill" and make a backhand shot at goal. In this way the two balls can be put through the goal whether by forehand, backhand or a combination of both.

Once the above is completed A and B can change positions and return down the ground with A in front of B.

Hooking sticks

This exercise could initially be done on foot with mini polo sticks and then perfected on ponies. This will avoid too much damage being done to your good full size polo sticks. The numbers taking part must be even, otherwise it is not important how many participate.

Let us imagine that there are six, *A*, *B*, *C* and *X*, *Y*, *Z*. The ball is placed in front of *A* with *X* to his right and just behind him. *B* and *Y* follow with *C* and *Z* placed as the third pair. All move together as *A* takes a full swing for an offside forehand. *X* hooks *A* and they both pass over the ball. *B* and *Y* repeat this as *Y* hooks *B*. They are followed by *C* who in turn is hooked by *Z*.

If all three hooks are successful the ball will still be stationary and all six players will have passed over it. Now all six should halt and turn round. Then *Z* comes back to the ball to be hooked by *C*. *Y* follows to be hooked by *B* and *X* should be hooked by *A*.

The idea is to practice hooking and not how to avoid being hooked. Therefore the striker must take a full swing and give his opposite number every chance to make a good hook.

The commentary is by the person making the hook: "Heel of stick head up, look at spot on opponent's stick, now hook."

Chapter 18

TACTICS "F"

TEAM PLAY

The four players in a team must have a special understanding. Besides knowing the rules of each position and the set pieces, they must know when to interchange and cover each other. Add to this a knowledge of what length of shot to expect from one another and which tactics will be used in certain situations. A few code words and signals should be planned. These are especially useful for hit-ins and penalties. Lastly, there has to be a will to play for the team first instead of seeking self-glory or selfishly chasing the ball around the ground. Sometimes this involves an unpopular change of positions, or a special task for one player who may thus lose some of the normal enjoyment in a match.

To achieve all the above the players need some form of preparation. A discussion together before each match is the minimum that should take place. At this the relative strengths and weaknesses of the opposition and themselves can be talked about. A pony plan for all the chukkas should be made. Knowledge of the opponent's pony power will help in the making of this. It is important that all the team do not start a chukka on their weakest pony. From this a general tactical plan could be made or a different scheme for each chukka prepared if there is a variation of pony power. If the team intend playing together for a season, or in several tournaments a long-term pony plan could be considered. Many teams have started a season well and then failed to gain further success because their ponies became overplayed and exhausted and therefore started playing badly.

If possible, some form of team practice should be added to any discussions. Playing together in club chukkas is one way. But a step further is to start the season by doing together some or all of the exercises explained in this book. If an experienced player or an ex-player can attend as coach even more value will be gained. Besides suggesting ways of combining better in the exercises he can help individuals with their striking and pony control if required. Furthermore, he might then be interested sufficiently to attend the matches and give vital team or individual advice between the chukkas and afterwards.

Normally the high-goal, or best player, thinks that he can play and coach at the same time. He may even resent the ideas of another person unless that person is someone whom he can respect and listen to. Then the results could be surprising.

A good player is apt to expect others to have his anticipation and reactions. When this does not happen not only does his play depreciate but the whole team suffers. He cannot fairly assess others in his team while producing the best anticipation and tactical hitting himself. His all round vision will be fully employed reacting to the actions of the seven other players on the ground. A non-playing coach should find it much easier to assess individual abilities and effectively mix them together.

A team sponsor sometimes compounds the problem by thinking that everything can be achieved by procuring the services of a top player. What he fails to realise is that without a separate coach the team will probably fail to achieve maximum cohesion. Also the sponsor's own chances of improvement are limited. He may win some cups but the majority of his positional role will be done for him by the top player, who has the ability to cover two positions for much of the time. The sponsor will gain from the experience of fast polo but lose much from his limited actual participation. Playing at a lower standard with a competent team player at No.3 plus a coach could improve team play and his personal ability much quicker. The higher standard could then be progressed to before too long.

A coach will also assist a team with pony plans both for individual matches and for the whole season.

As already suggested hours of time can be saved and probable damage to, or over exertion of, ponies avoided by practising on foot. Many people will not believe that there is value in working with the mini sticks until they actually do it. Then they see that not only are the striking techniques exactly the same but that there is an opportunity to practice all the tactical situations in slow motion.

MINI GROUND

This is polo played on foot.

Striking

You will be surprised to find that accurate hitting with a mini stick when on foot is not as easy as might be expected. The mini stick should be between thirty and thirty-six inches long. Although it is unlikely that you will hit late, the other problems related to hitting from a pony will be encountered. Therefore the same five rules must be applied for all the shots.

You place yourself to the ball. Remember the stick and hand position. Use the shoulders by putting the relevant foot to the ball. Your head goes down to the sweet spot. You follow through with the back of the hand.

Ball

Unless you are by yourself it is advisable not to use a normal polo ball. Not only will the ball travel too far, but in a confined space there is a considerable danger that someone will be hurt when struck by the ball. Many alternative types of rubber or soft balls can be used but best of all is one of soft foam. This is very soft and cannot damage people or windows. However hard it is struck the speed of the ball will relate to people rather than ponies moving about the ground. Tretorn and Pellican are two of the makers of this type of ball.

Ground

Dimensions are optional, however too short a ground will prevent positional play and tactics being realistic while too long will make defence too easy and fail to simulate the normal events of a chukka. Ideally a mini ground should be sixty yards by thirty yards.

In this case each 30 yard line would be six yards from the back line and the 60 yard line would be a further six yards from the 30 yard line. The goal width is also optional, but the narrower the better. This will make participants use correct striking techniques if they wish to score. Therefore one and a half yards is the width suggested.

The ideal surface is grass which has been cut as a lawn. Otherwise any flat, reasonably firm, type of ground can be used.

Speed of play

Again, this is optional and can be varied to make the proceedings more entertaining. Obviously the alternatives are to walk or to run. The former is the best for the majority of the time. When walking all aspects of the game can be simulated in slow motion. Control is simple and all faults are easily highlighted. The ball-chaser is clearly exposed and fouls are not difficult to detect. To run is a foul and therefore no one can take advantage of being a fast runner to chase the ball. Instead the key factor will be anticipation which can be achieved through carrying out the five rules of tactics. Another dimension can be achieved by using the rope which all the players of one team have to hold. We discuss this in more detail later.

EXERCISES

In previous chapters it was mentioned that much time on the full size ground with ponies can be saved if the exercises are done on foot beforehand. Any doubt as to the sequence of events within the exercise can be cleared up. Techniques and ways of conforming to each other can be explained, practised and repeated many times. Because accuracy is that much easier to achieve everyone can partake in all the movements of an exercise. Thereby they can learn the lessons that are incorporated even if they are not proficient enough, at this stage, to do the exercise correctly on a pony. If the exercises involving a whole team are successfully carried out on the mini ground there will be much more confidence when they are repeated on ponies.

Conducting exercises on foot

The instructor will hold these exercises on the mini ground. He should ensure that everyone starts in the correct positions so that the same action as when mounted on ponies is simulated. Participants should be encouraged to commentate throughout. Either the words that have been suggested or their own thoughts can be used. This is guaranteed to speed up the action. In most exercises you should try to finish by scoring goals. The application of that final shot is so important. If you cannot score on the mini ground how can you hope to do so on a pony in a big ground? Many players are reasonably accurate with every shot except that one at goal. The extra pressure upsets the timing. This can be relieved considerably by successful practice.

Lengths of shot should be sensible and suitable to assist the success of the exercise. This especially applies to a person "linking to goal". Here a controlled full shot of five to six yards will allow the process of linking to be repeated several times in one length of the ground.

The rope exercise

This is the best possible way to demonstrate how the team can remain in correct positions during a movement from one end of the ground to the other. It will clearly show the requirement for exact adjustments which will maintain four players in four positions. It can and should be done by a group of beginners during their first day of instruction. Even more experienced players will benefit from the rope exercise which is enjoyable and can be most amusing.

The length of the rope should be approximately twelve yards. Two knots should be tied at the four and eight yard marks. No.1 and No.4 hold the two ends of the rope and No.2 and No.3 the two knots. The team starts at one end of the ground with No.3 standing on the goal line with the ball placed beside him. The rope is taut with No.4 behind the line and No.1 and No.2 in front of it. All move together using "all round vision" to ensure that the rope remains taut throughout. No.1 heads for the left hand goal

post at the far end. No.4 takes the first shot, No.3 the second, No.2 the third and then No.1 shoots at goal. After this all can turn round and take up positions before returning down the ground. This time the roles could be reversed by putting No.4 as No.1, No.3 as No.2 and so on.

If all the shots are accurate in direction and length there will be very little adjustment required other than keeping the rope taut. But if any shot goes to the left or right all four players should adjust to the left or right. No.1 moves to a position where the left hand goal post, the ball and himself form a straight line. No.2, No.3 and No.4 adjust to make a direct extension to this line. This means that No.4 has to move the furthest to the left or right. Thus, each successive player will have a straight shot in the direction of goal whether or not the previous hit was accurate. By keeping the rope taut while making any lateral adjustments may involve changes in pace. This is a realistic part of team polo. So often one player is too close to, or too far back from, the man in front of him because he fails to alter his speed.

Conduct of a game

Throw-ins, hit-ins, penalties and all the tactics we have discussed can be carried out in the same way as on the big ground with ponies. There are only two basic differences in the applications of the rules. The first, speed of play, has already been discussed and the second is the method of riding-off.

Let us presume that you are only allowed to walk and that to run is a foul. The umpire can control this by deciding when walking with exaggerated long strides or too fast should be counted as running. Then a hit from the spot can be awarded against the culprit. The temptation to run is difficult for many to resist. But the majority will cease doing it if the umpire is strict. A few people are such bad ball-chasers that they can never be cured. There are two ways of dealing with such a person. Either tie his feet together so that he has to hop or make his team hold the rope while playing.

For the ride-off it is imperative that pushing

Mini ground

(Above) *The rope exercise. All the team has adjusted to the* left *while No.3 takes the second shot*
(Opposite page, above) *All the team has adjusted to the* right *while No.2 takes the third shot*
(Opposite page, below) *No.1 is still opposite the left-hand goal post while taking the fourth shot*

and the use of force is forbidden. Both must be punished with penalties otherwise there will be chaos and very little benefit will be gained. So how can you win a ride-off? By early closing and making it quite clear to the umpire and the relative opponent that you did it first. Calling out "early closing" while placing your shoulder in front of the opponent is the best method. Unfortunately it may also be necessary to let your elbow go in front of his chest. But only if it is so close that you have to prove to an over competitive opponent that you were first. Otherwise keep the elbows down and your opponent should accept the ride-off and allow you to control the pace and the direction of you both.

If you lose the ride-off you should consider two factors. First, that you ought to stay in position and not risk breaking the tactical rule of four players in four positions; second that your actions should simulate the actual polo played on ponies. With this in mind you have two alternatives. To continue with your opponent in the ride-off or to stop and completely detach from him. If you continue you have a further choice. To stay behind his shoulder ready to take control if the play changes direction or to attempt to re-win the ride-off after a few strides. The latter might be achieved by detaching for a second and then recovering one yard of ground before closing again, this time, with your shoulder in front.

Numbers in teams

Four against four, as in normal polo with ponies, is the best way to play, learn the lessons from and simulate real polo. But if there are less than eight people available it is still possible to play, enjoy and learn from a game. Three against three, two a side or even a single between two people have some training value.

With two a side one player must obey the rules for being in front of the barrier and the other for being behind it. Therefore, when there is an interchange both players will experience crossing the barrier and taking on the different responsibilities that this involves.

One against one is good training for

"keeping the back door shut". At the same time it invites you to find a way of getting past an opponent, or how to win a ride-off when coming from behind. These can only be attempted after some preparatory manoeuvring is done in order to set up a certainty situation.

Umpiring

Everyone should have a chance to umpire. The line of the ball and ways of crossing it are exactly the same as when on ponies. Having to decide when fouls are committed by others must help you to discipline yourself in this matter. Ideally an instructor who is not playing should be the umpire on the mini ground. He can see all fouls clearly. The misuse of the mini stick is more than tempting to some people.

The game can be restarted with all the players in selected positions on the ground. He can also ensure that all the different penalties are awarded so that they may be practiced even if it makes one team complain of unfairness!

If necessary the umpire and instructor can be one of the players. With a whistle round his neck he can play and control the game at the same time.

Team on the rope

One team can play while holding the rope. This means that they will have the disadvantage of being unable to interchange. This could be countered by allowing them to run while their opponents can only walk. If the rope is kept taut no one can go out of position to chase the ball. In fact the whole team must remain in their original four positions.

For the second chukka the rope could be given to the other team to hold and the situations reversed. Besides scoring goals there could be a competition in which the team with the most interchanges when not holding the rope is the winner. This is a good training exercise for both teams. The interchanges will have to be created and the opponents will have to adjust their marking accordingly.

Chapter 19

POLO PONIES

The most important characteristic of a pony is temperament. Unless the pony is calm and sensible there are certain to be problems of control in a fast game. A soft mouth making a pony easy to stop and turn is also vital.

Good conformation will add to the chances of a pony remaining sound in wind and limb for many years. At the same time a pony should be of the appropriate size to carry the weight of any would be player. A good wide front and strong quarters are a necessary attribute for supporting the weight of heavy men.

It is most important that the correct grade of pony is matched to the ability of a player. It is fatal if a beginner tries to play on a high-goal pony.

For many years the majority of polo ponies have come from the Argentine. They are the most reliable ponies because they come from a line of polo playing dams and breeding that was not interrupted by the two world wars. Also much Argentinian farmland is excellent for rearing ponies.

Recently there has been an influx of good ponies from New Zealand where the standard of play and pony production is improving rapidly. Otherwise, for ponies of substance, the only other countries are the United States, Britain and Australia. The Arabs continue to breed many lovely ponies who can play well amongst themselves but not when matched against bigger ponies.

PURCHASING

There are many considerations when

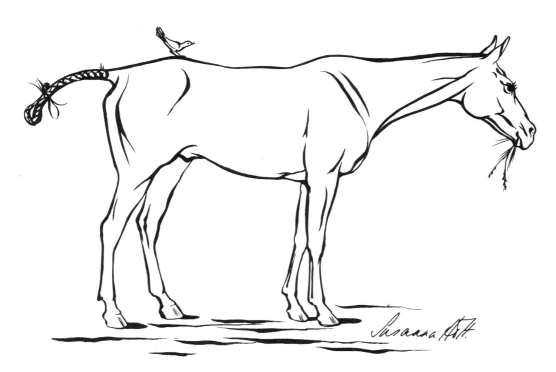

The right type to buy

purchasing a pony. How much you can afford, availability and your standard of polo are three of the primary ones. Does the pony stop and turn and will it allow you to hit the ball are just some of the other questions that should be asked.

However, the most important factor of all is one of personal taste which is hard to define. You should feel that there is an accord between you and the pony during play. Therefore, it is vital that you do play a pony before making a purchase. Merely to see somebody else playing the pony or to ride the pony without a trial in a chukka is seldom sufficient. Some ponies will be brilliant at schooling and stick and ball, but lack courage in a chukka. Others are excellent for good players in high-goal polo but far too excitable for a lesser player in low-goal polo. It is impossible to find out these points without playing a pony in a chukka of similar standard to the polo that is planned for the current season.

Beware of the ponies which are being sold because they have a particular fault. Shying off the ball and difficulty in stopping are two examples. A beginner has enough to learn without having to worry about problems with his pony. It is unlikely that you will be able to cure them. Knowledge of the pony's history may help you to avoid this. Owners who had the pony for one season only are suspect unless you are certain that there is a genuine reason for sale.

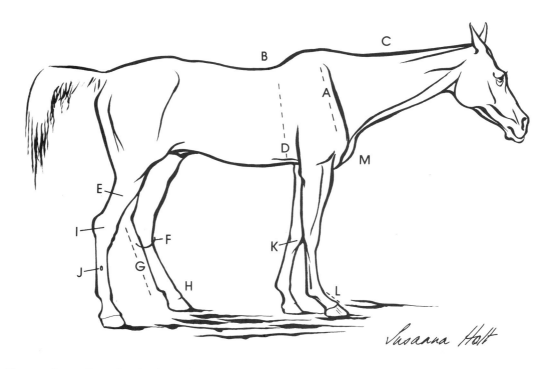

Reasons for caution when buying a pony
A = *Straight shoulder;* **B** = *Hollow back;* **C** = *"U" neck;* **D** = *Shallow girth;* **E** = *Narrow second thigh;* **F** = *Narrow hooked hindleg;* **G** = *Long and weak hindleg;* **H** = *Bone growth on pastern;* **I** = *Capped hock;* **J** = *Lack of bone;* **K** = *Over at the knee;* **L** = *Long pastern;* **M** = *Narrow in front*

If the owners have brought them from abroad with a view to selling them as a straight business transaction it is a different situation. Therefore, ponies that are new and ones that have played several seasons are the best. The ponies who started in high-goal polo and then, as age slowed them up, came down through medum- to low-goal polo, could be ideal for beginners.

There is an outside possibility that a pony has a fault because of a simple reason which the seller has failed to spot. For example, the wrong or badly fitting tack can upset even the best pony. Sharp teeth and bad shoeing are other reasons for a pony playing poorly. If you can diagnose such a situation it may give you the opportunity to make a successful cheap purchase. However, be careful that there is not another reason, far more deep rooted, that is causing the pony to be awkward.

Another danger is that a pony may play brilliantly for you during the first five or six minutes of a chukka after which he becomes difficult. You may be so pleased with those five or six minutes that you discount the end of the chukka. If the chukka never opens out sufficiently to give a test of stamina that same pony may not be exposed. Therefore, be certain that the pony is tested for endurance and do not accept excuses from the seller until you are satisfied from your own experience.

Once you have decided that the pony plays well enough for you it will be time for a veterinary examination. If you employ a vet with a reputation for examining polo ponies there is no problem. But beware that some drugs or stimulants have not been used. The vet who is not experienced with polo ponies may possibly be fooled if this has happened by the tricks of a seller. It is advisable to have the pony examined on two different occasions. Once, when the pony is cold and has not been warmed up or exercised, and again after the pony has taken violent exercise, such as a gallop, or has actually played a fast chukka.

A further consideration concerns the use of X-rays. This is an expensive way of ensuring that there are no bone diseases in the pony's legs and feet. Naturally it is money well spent

if it saves you from spending several thousand pounds on a pony with navicular disease. However, an experienced polo vet may be able to advise you on relevant matters such as age and hoof shape. From this you may think that an X-ray is not necessary. Nevertheless, if in doubt, stipulate that any deal is subject to the results of an X-ray.

Also, there are a few undesirable pony vices which would never be detected in the normal course of trying out a pony or during a veterinary inspection. What are these and how can you check if they exist? A pony that is difficult to load into a horse box can cause you endless problems. Other ponies are bad travellers and may injure themselves while badly upsetting any companions in that horse box. A kicker is unacceptable as he is dangerous on the ground, at exercise and when out at grass with other ponies. A pony that will not lead from another can be a nuisance, although if he is the only one of a group with this defect he can always be ridden and never led. There are those who refuse to be tied up and therefore have to be held or permanently watched instead of being left in the pony lines. Then there are the stable vices, such as weaving and crib-biting. Besides suffering themselves from these antics the ponies may easily be copied by others in the same stable yard. A pony may be very difficult to shoe or even need tranquilising before a blacksmith may start to work.

There are many different ways of checking if these vices exist. The first rule is not to make a purchase in a hurry. Try to see the pony at least twice, preferably three times, before finalising the deal. A preliminary inspection, playing and then a veterinary examination could all happen on separate days and in different locations. On each occasion watch the pony with the possibility of the above mentioned vices in mind. With luck you may see him with other ponies, when tied up, while being led and even being loaded into a horse box.

If possible visit the stables or ask a vet to do so and, when you do, pick up the pony's legs yourself and observe his reactions.

Anyway, why not ask the vendor if the pony has any vices? But this is of little use if the deal is already completed. Perhaps you can add a few contingencies to the deal which will protect you from purchasing a pony with any vices. Otherwise, make some investigations and ask other people about the history of the pony and the reputation of the seller. One or more of these simple precautions may one day save you from an unfortunate purchase.

BREEDING

There are many risks and expenses involved in the process of breeding polo ponies though it is a pleasant way of giving an old faithful mare a few extra years of life. Also a mare who breaks down at an early age may reimburse you with some good offspring. But people should not allow sentimentality to cloud their judgement or they may end up with a reduced bank balance and some worthless young animals.

The following thoughts merely touch on a subject which is a complex one. An experienced breeder of polo ponies may have much to add and should be consulted.

The mare

The chances of breeding a good pony are much higher if the dam has played polo. It seems that some experience is automatically passed on, which makes the training of a young pony quicker and easier. Where the dam has not played then often the offspring will flatter to deceive. Initially the training may go well but once any real question is asked a strong resistance can be encountered. Otherwise what are the qualities that should be looked for in a mare? The first and foremost is a quiet temperament. This is almost certain to be passed on to the progeny. The pony that is over excited is the hardest to train. The calm, good natured, pony will accept the necessary training and learn polo schooling more readily.

Secondly, good confirmation in a dam will probably ensure that the offspring are sound in wind and limb. Once again any physical fault in the mother may be passed on.

Speed is an important quality if ensuing young stock are going to play in good-class polo. However this ingredient could be added by a stallion if the dam is excellent in every other way.

The stallion

The safest way of breeding is to procure the services of a stallion that has been regularly and successfully used for polo mares. However, such a stallion may not be available in a specific place and an experiment sometimes has to be made.

Polo pony breeders have experimented with many different kinds of stallions. Variations in height and breed have produced surprising and different results. Once again temperament is a key factor. But size is important as ponies which are too big or too small are useless and worthless for polo. There are thoroughbred horses who although are over sixteen hands, will normally give a dam a progeny of her own size. This may well produce extra strength and speed making their offspring brilliant and valuable. But there will always be a risk that they will grow too big.

Other considerations

The time of foaling should be planned where possible. If it is too late into the summer a year of polo may have to be forfeited. When breaking and training should be starting the owner may find the youngster is not sufficiently developed to take the strain and stress of being ridden. Therefore, you have to wait until the following year. If the mare is perfectly sound there is no reason why she cannot be played after being covered by the stallion for the whole of that season. It is also possible to play a mare before her foal has been weaned from her. This could start after two to three months from the date of foaling. Some people take the foal to the polo ground, others leave it in a stable at home. Whichever method is chosen it is important that before this happens the foal is left alone on one or two occasions.

TRAINING

Breaking is the name for the first training that a pony receives. It should be done by an expert who is normally a professional. If it is not done correctly there is little chance that the pony will ever be able to play polo properly. In Argentina there is a profession called *Domador*. These men do nothing else except break potential polo ponies. Their methods can be rather cruel and the aim of completely dominating a pony is generally achieved. As a result the Argentinian pony can easily take fright from any unexpected movement done on the ground. After this, the pony is handed over to a groom or player who carries out the training which leads up to the introduction to polo.

In Britain one man will probably be in charge of both breaking and subsequent training stages which are therefore joined together. The trainer introduces a polo stick very soon after the pony is first ridden.

The programme between the first day of breaking and the first match chukka of polo is extensive and itself requires a book. Suffice to say that the end product must be a pony that accepts and answers all the demands of the player for manoeuverability, control and speed. The ability to change speed both violently and minimally without fighting with the player is itself priceless.

Once a pony is playing regularly it is important that schooling continues between matches. This is not necessarily done to improve the pony but to maintain a standard which otherwise can drop very quickly. Why? Because during a match ponies may be hurt in one or more ways by their riders or by other ponies. As a result they may be remembering this when the next match is played and will try to avoid suffering a similar experience. But if between matches the ponies are allowed to enjoy a school they should start the next game with the memory of the schooling foremost in their minds. In this way ponies can be kept content and playing well throughout a season.

Schooling between matches should not be devoted to stick and ball only because this is mainly for the benefit of the rider. The exercises which have been explained in the polo riding chapters are an excellent way of allowing the ponies to enjoy themselves while being schooled. If they go badly during any of these exercises the riders should investigate the reason. Teeth, legs and correct fitting of tack are the first things to look at. If none of these are responsible the problem will probably be one of confidence. In this case the relevant exercise should be repeated several times until done well. If necessary go back to the walk before increasing speed to that at which the problem was met.

Schooling will also help to maintain pony fitness and strength for all the twists and turns that are demanded when playing.

PLAYING THE PONY

How much polo should a pony play in one week, one month, or in one season? This is a question which cannot be given a general answer because ponies vary so much in their physical ability and endurance. But there are various considerations that can and should be applied to all ponies.

The pony is not a machine and it must be wrong to expect any one pony to play two chukkas three times a week throughout a season. It is a false economy, though unfortunately applied by many players, that a pony must play every polo day regardless of other factors in order to justify the costs of upkeep. Admittedly some ponies thrive on plenty of polo and others will play better in the second chukka of a match than they did in the first. Also it is a mistake to give a pony an odd practice chukka here and there and then expect a fabulous performance in a match or a tournament.

Therefore, a compromise between over- and under-playing should be planned as is relevant to the characteristics of each pony. Playing two chukkas in matches may be unavoidable if a player only has two ponies. In this case practice chukkas in mid-season should be limited if there are matches every weekend. Either the practice day should be completely avoided or the ponies just given one chukka each according to the factors that need considering.

If a player has three or more ponies he should try not to over-play the best ones regardless of other factors. On practise days chukkas can be used as an extra school for any pony that has developed a fault. For example, if a pony prefers turning to the left the player can consistently turn him to the right. Also a player can himself practise a particular shot at which he is weak or instead of riding-off he can practise hooking sticks throughout a chukka. Anyway it is best to play the majority of practice chukkas in ''third gear'' allowing the extra speed of ''top gear'' to be in reserve for the match days that are important.

After playing, inspection of ponies should take place to look for injuries. The following day another check should be carried out as it may reveal some damage that has taken time to come to the surface. In many cases quick and effective treatment will prevent a simple injury from becoming a serious one. If a pony is playing again before the problem is spotted the damage may be compounded and the pony lost from polo for a long time. Legs, mouth and back are the most important places to watch.

Chapter 20

POLO PREPARATION

To be ready for the first polo match of the season requires more than a little thought. Besides preparing ponies, the correct clothes, equipment and polo sticks must be assembled. The fun of playing polo can be enormously increased if the problems are reduced by a little planning.

CLOTHES AND EQUIPMENT

White breeches are easy to buy, but you should ensure that they fit properly otherwise there can be much discomfort and sometimes leg sores. Boots should be kept clean and soft during the off-season. There is no rule as to type of boot but it is not ethical to wear black ones. This is because black polish does not wash off breeches whereas brown does. It is advisable to have boots that come right up to the knee for the sake of leg protection.

Gloves are important. Some players always wear them, others have them in their pocket ready for an emergency while there are less clever players who do not own any. If you have to play in the wet without gloves it will be difficult to hold the reins properly. In hot weather it will be the same when the ponies break out and the reins are covered in their sweat. In any weather a blister may suddenly appear on either hand caused by holding the reins or the stick and a glove will be vital to prevent further discomfort and damage.

No one is allowed to play polo without wearing a hard hat known as a polo helmet. Over the years the shape, colour and design has been changing. Originally everyone wore white in the shape of the Indian topee. Today many different colours are seen, sometimes there is a mixture on one hat and the shape varies between a hunting cap to the latest which resembles a motor cycle helmet. For me the most important factor is that the helmet is comfortable. The protection required is two fold: from being struck by a ball and from falling off the pony head-first on to the ground. The two necessities clash because a face guard attached to a helmet may protect the eyes, nose and mouth from a flying ball yet it can cause extra damage to them and the neck if there is a fall. Also the face guard can make a helmet too heavy for comfort and possibly interfere with all round vision. However the choice belongs to the player who can, of course, experiment with different hats and face guards. At present the majority of the top players do not wear face guards yet there are several people, with permanent scars, who wish they had.

Knee pads are optional. There are few things more painful than when one bony knee hits another. Often it is the opponent who benefits most from your knee pad. However the vast majority of players do wear them. There are several different types and once again comfort must be the main consideration when a selection is made.

A polo whip is a vital piece of equipment. You cannot expect to get the best from your pony without one. Unless you encounter the exception which is a pony that is "whip shy". A slap on the neck or a hard stroke behind your left leg onto the flanks of the pony may one day win a match by enabling you to score a goal or prevent an opponent from shooting. It is important to have the correct length. Too short can be ineffective while too long will interfere with the nearside shot and unintentionally tickle a wretched pony at the wrong moment.

Spurs are optional but if worn should not be sharp. Beginner riders beware. Many players wear spurs without knowing how to use them and find themselves being run away with by a pony which is normally quiet and easy. There are some good ponies which will play badly if the rider uses spurs on them, but the majority will benefit from them if applied correctly. Then there are ponies who will develop bad habits if the rider does not always play in spurs while others may benefit if they are only used in matches and not in practice games. Therefore spurs should be a part of a player's equipment which is always taken to the ground and used selectively.

The tack for the ponies should have been put away at the end of the previous season, clean and oiled. Now the oil is cleaned off and the leather maintained in a soft condition through the application of saddle soap. The saddles should be thoroughly checked to see that a tree is not broken and that there are no lumps or sharp edges which could hurt the back of the pony. Also the fitting of the pommel on the withers of the pony should be examined. Girths and leathers require special attention to see that there are no weaknesses which could later cause a break to take place. Bridles ought to be carefully fitted to ponies. For the bit to be a 100% comfortable in the mouth the cheek strap must be the correct length. The bits themselves should be the size that suits a pony best and must be checked for sharp edges. Nose and forehead bands may need adjusting and the correct length of martingale is important. Curb chains ought to be fitted to ensure that they can operate correctly on the hooks. Too loose or too tight a chain can give problems.

Boots and bandages need inspecting and fitting to check that buckles, straps and all materials are in good condition. Badly fitted boots or bandages that no longer give support for legs will soon cause leg problems.

POLO STICKS

It is difficult to do justice to your ponies and yourself if you do not have good polo sticks. The length, weight and stiffness are all very personal matters. Only through experimenting and patience will the best solution to them be found. Even then as your polo career continues you may want to change one or more of them.

It is ideal if whatever the height of pony you play you use the same length of stick. It is simple and costs are reduced. If you are able to do this without any difficulty it will mean that you have a better eye and co-ordination to hit a ball than the majority of players. The length of stick that suits you best will depend on two factors, accuracy and length of shot.

The longer the stick the further the shot if you have complete control over the swing. Therefore I would suggest once you are confident of carrying out the correct techniques of striking with a polo stick whose length is 49 or 50 inches you can then experiment with longer ones to see if accuracy can be maintained. You will quickly discover a length which is too long because perfect co-ordination is unattainable with it. Then you should revert to a stick one inch shorter.

After that, further tests can be made with different weights of stick head and varying degrees of stiffness in the cane. A heavy head and a whippy cane will be most effective for distance if you can control such a stick. Most people cannot, neither do they like a very stiff cane. There will be little difficulty in knowing when you pick up a stick which is perfect for you. You will feel the fabulous sensation of effortless co-ordination. Then you should take that special polo stick to a stick maker and ask him to copy it. The famous Raymond Turner at Salters in Aldershot is brilliant at doing just that.

He or other experts can also advise you which shape of heads to use if you explain the standard of polo that you expect to play in. Basically the cigar is the best for accuracy because it has the largest surface while the RNPA will give the greatest assistance for lofting the ball. The skene and various others made to order can be a sensible compromise between the two.

However you may find that on ponies of different size you cannot use the same length of stick. This becomes apparent when on smaller ponies you regularly hit the ground and on bigger ponies you top the ball or make embarrassing air shots. In this case you ought to purchase sticks of three different lengths to cover all circumstances. For example, 49, 50 and 51 or maybe 50, 51 and 52 if you can be accurate with the latter. In an emergency the stirrup leather can be altered up or down instead of changing sticks but as a regular practice this would interfere with pony control.

In the off-season it is advisable to take all

your sticks to a stick-maker. They will all require straightening and balancing besides any other necessary repairs or renewals to heads, canes and handles. At home they should be kept in an atmosphere which is not too hot or damp. When at the polo ground, sticks will deteriorate if left in the sun or lying in wet grass.

Finally, you will save yourself many problems if you have a system of marking your sticks. For example, one or more colours could be painted on the cane just below the handle in order to prove ownership. If you have different lengths of stick a colour code should be put on the cane just above the head. For example, red for 51 and green for 50, etc., will make identification simple for yourself and an unfortunate wife or helper who answers the cry of ''stick, stick'' in the middle of a game.

PONIES

Assuming that the same ponies as were played in the previous season are now out in a field just before the beginning of the new season, there are several points which should be thought about.

It is essential to plan a programme of worming which will ensure no deterioration of conditions. Do not wait for the first signs of worms. Instead, use a recognised product and ensure regular dosing following the manufacturer's instructions. Any dosage given should always be recorded in a diary.

Any signs of leg wear should be treated. In fact if in doubt, between seasons, once all the swelling and cuts are completely healed, some form of blister should be applied.

Depending on the climate, and availability of grass, extra feeding ought to be given during the winter. The aim should be that there is some weight to lose when exercise first begins before the new season. Hay or oaten straw can achieve this and if some hard food like oats or nuts are added during the last months of grass, it will be easier and quicker to reach and maintain full fitness. A large area in which to roam at grass will also assist when the process of getting the pony fit begins.

Annual injections against 'flu and tetanus must be given. When exercise is about to start, before a season, is as good a time as any and the necessary documentary evidence should be obtained.

Shoeing is straight forward as long as there is a good blacksmith in your area. Otherwise it is important to continually check that the clinches are down and that the fitting of the shoes are correct. The first set of shoes normally need not be prepared for studs or have corkings fitted, in order that you will have more scope as to where the ponies can be exercised.

Clipping is optional and the necessity for doing it will depend on several factors, especially the type of weather expected. A complete clip and rugging in the stable is the easiest way to keep a pony clean and prevent unnecessary sweating as exercise speeds up. The trace clip is a good compromise, which dispenses with the use of rugs and allows the pony to be left out in the day, or even over night, if desirable at any time. The only advantage of not clipping is that the summer coat will come through earlier and look that little bit better. But the grooming will be very hard work initially.

The amount of food and exercise is a matter which can be discussed endlessly. There are many alternatives all of which can be successful. The combination of both is the vital factor. Too much of one and too little of another is a common fault which ends with many problems including lack of pony control and weakness in condition. In this respect the preparation of a high-goal pony is entirely different to the rest. Why? Because the speed of play is so much faster and gallops from one end of the ground to the other happen that much more often than in other polo. As a result stamina of extreme proportions has to be built up through extensive exercise and large feeds.

In ordinary polo the initial exercising could be as little as a half hour per day with cantering commencing after only a few days. But when the actual polo playing begins the ponies will require many days of slowish chukkas before they are asked to give their all in a match. In this way much of the time spent in getting the pony fit is done on the polo ground while playing. Another alternative is to exercise twice a day giving larger feeds. The ponies could be one and a half to two hours out of the stable and will then be ready for fast chukkas when the season starts. Obviously there are many other exercising programmes which fit in somewhere between these two extremes. The old teaching of six weeks on the roads has been thrown out of the window. This used to involve a steady increase in trotting ending up with several miles a day. In Argentina I formed the impression that the trot barely existed. Polo ponies in work seem to go straight from a walk to a canter. However the dangers of leg injuries, girth gall and sore backs is increased. These unnecessary injuries can be avoided with a little thought, especially if riding and leading is the method of exercising employed. A variation of which pony is ridden and which is lead is vital, to ensure that all become reaccustomed to the pressure of saddle and girth after the winter lay off.

The amount of schooling, plus stick and ball, done before playing the first chukka of a season must depend on the characteristics of each individual pony. The old experienced pony, who knows more about polo than his rider, may need none. The young inexperienced pony will probably require many sessions. The training already mentioned is a good guide as to what can be done in some of the sessions.

Chapter 21

THE RULES AND UMPIRING

It is unbelievable how many players have never read the rules. Of those that have the majority seldom revise them. The Hurlingham Polo Association rules are well laid out, simple and self explanatory. The only other countries that have written their own book of rules are the United States of America and Argentina. The latter and the H.P.A. vary in very little. The Americans have several different ways of fouling and an ever changing system of awarding penalties.

Wherever you are about to play, the rules that are applicable ought to be read before each season and especially if you are visiting another country. It is hard enough not to make fouls when you do know the rules, but there are many situations where ignorance of them will bring about the award of further penalties against your team. As in every sport rules are constantly being changed as a result of peoples experiences and with the desire to avoid a repeat of some unfortunate incident. How can you conform if you are not fully up to date? The game of polo is dangerous enough without having players who are not aware of some rules.

Sooner or later you will be asked to umpire. The sooner the better as this will help you to understand the rules, besides giving you an on the spot insight into what can and cannot be done in a polo match. However, you may be made to feel very stupid if you do not know the rules. Normally there are two umpires and your partner may be able to cover for your ignorance. Yet there are situations which require umpires to be watching from two different positions and at times your partner may not be able to interpret a particular rule from where he is. There are times when your partner is positioned to judge the line but momentarily loses his sight of the

play—having to get out of the way of a player, being on the turn or having the scene blocked from view by a pony in front of him. Whatever the cause, if there is a foul, you will have to blow the whistle and award a penalty.

On many occasions it is desirable that one of you is behind the line of the ball and the other to the side of it. In this way one umpire can see if anyone crosses the line, when it is a foul to do so, and the other umpire can see any mis-deed committed with the stick such as across the legs of an opponent's pony and any tricks, such as swinging the head of the pony into an opponent's back to discredit a perfectly legal ride-off. It is important that both umpires are highly mobile and never allow distance to impair their judgement. If each umpire has one side line and one back line as his responsibility, the chances of covering all eventualities are good. Therefore at a hit-in the umpire who is responsible for the relevant back line will initially be able to follow the striker and clearly see any meets or crosses that are a foul. The other umpire being at, or near, his side line can see any transgression with the stick. However, one long angled backhander from the team opposing the hit-in will probably bring the latter to be behind the line and the former to be to the side of it. Also, at any time during play, when the game suddenly changes direction the two umpires will probably exchange roles and, therefore, in many situations you cannot rely on your partner to interpret the rules for you.

The best way to maintain good concentration as an umpire is to continually commentate to yourself "that is the line". When a foul occurs it should then be obvious who had the right of way, even if you do not know which way the teams at that moment are playing. This is not important. Why? Because if necessary it is simple to ask one of the players "which way is your team playing?" Once this fact is established you will be able to consider the gravity of the foul and the appropriate penalty to award.

There are three main factors which decide the penalty to be imposed—where it happened, the direction of play at the time and how serious the foul was. For example, if the team fouled is in defence near the middle of the ground and the offence is minor, the hit will be from the centre. But if that team had been in attack a 60 yard penalty would probably be awarded. If the foul occurred near the 60 yard line the former would merit a 60 yard penalty and the latter probably a 40 yard penalty.

A further factor is whether the goal is actually threatened or not. A foul near the side line and the back line by the defending team does not necessarily merit a 30 yard penalty if the ball was travelling towards the side line and there was no possibility of the attacking team setting up a goal at that moment.

One of the commonest fouls that often goes unpunished is intimidation. Until recently the United States did not even mention the word in their rules. In England certain forms of intimidation are well-known. For example, a player riding at right angles towards an opponent giving the impression that he will not stop. But some less obvious forms of intimidation are invariably not detected. A player who is rapidly closing up on an opponent who knows that the ball is still running just behind him but that he will foul if he checks to wait for it. The player is wondering if the opponent realises this or not while bravely attempting to concentrate on making the next shot. At the last moment the opponent allows his pony to move minutely sideways and towards the ball resulting in the player taking his eye off the ball after he has begun to swing the stick. In fact as an umpire you can easily spot this if you have just said to yourself ''there is the line'' instead of thinking ''will he hit the ball?''. It is fatal if an umpire allows himself to become involved in the tactics of the game. When detected, intimidation must always be appropriately dealt with by an umpire.

Unfortunately there are many tricks which the high handicap players can do in order to confuse an umpire. It is strange that these are not highlighted by the authorities in any of the Polo Associations. The worst of these is, possibly, when two players are meeting each other from opposite directions and both at the outset are legally ''on the main road''. The better player realising that his opponent is going to arrive at the ball first very slightly changes his line of approach. Immediately an inattentive umpire will be fooled into thinking that the opponent is rushing in to hit without joining the exact line. If instead of presuming that the better player was correct, the umpire said to himself ''there is the line'' this unfair ploy would be detected. Besides keeping concentration this system of commentating ''the line'' throughout also prevents an umpire from only ball-watching. This fault allows dirty tricks, such as swinging the head of the pony into the back of the opponent, to succeed with the intention of fabricating a foul instead of itself being castigated for dangerous play.

If the two umpires disagree on who is the culprit, or about which penalty to award, they can consult with an official who is in the stand or centrally placed on the side line. The Hurlingham Polo Association call him ''the referee'', the United States Polo Association describe him as ''the third man'' and the Argentinians aptly name him ''the Arbitrator''. He has to devote an hour or more watching a game with intense concentration. Often he is wasting his time because the umpires never consult with him. In fact, his authority could be increased to assist the umpires and provide a better and more constructive way of controlling the game. In the Hurlingham Polo Association umpires are graded as ''A'', ''B'' and ''C''. Therefore if the third official is an ''A'' why not empower him to call the umpires to his position between chukkas in order to discuss their decisions, positioning and any other relevant factors? On occasions a point of extreme value could be highlighted to assist the umpires in their task for the remainder of the game. For example, the best player on the ground may be misusing his talent and experience to mislead and confuse the umpires in their interpretation of the rules. The umpires would have nothing to lose by listening and could assess the advice given according to the known experience and ability of this third official. Young and inexperienced umpires could only gain and learn for the future especially if the referee was selected with this aspect in mind.

This wonderful game of polo can be so easily spoilt by bad umpiring. People spend considerable amounts of time and money and travel long distances to play. They deserve to find the best possible and fairest arrangements for the conduct of their game. This is seldom feasible if a visiting team encounter two home umpires. The cynics would say that the game was being played by four against six. Realistically two umpires from the same club as one of the teams will find it very difficult not to be biased in some way. Whether consciously or unconsciously their decisions and judgements between a player they know well and strangers will be at times clouded. Therefore, the possibility of both teams feeling that they were justly treated is greatly improved if at least one umpire is in no way connected to the home team or if the umpires are from two different clubs.

On one occasion I was disappointed to watch a team of foreign visitors play in a fourteen goal tournament against one of the home teams. Not only were the two umpires from the home club but they both were members of a high-goal team in which the patron of this home team played. They made decisions which appeared to have some bias in favour of the home team. The foreigners were perfect sportsmen throughout and betrayed no sign of annoyance in defeat at the ground. Afterwards one of them mentioned in the mildest possible form that the umpiring had been poor. There were many other players who were from other clubs and were available for umpiring. Therefore, the situation is totally unnecessary and a simple edict from the authority would prevent a club secretary from allowing such a situation to occur.

Whatever the faults of other umpires, players and officials you can help in many situations if you know and understand the rules. Firstly, by umpiring well and, secondly, as a player, by understanding the problems of an umpire which, in most cases, will allow you to accept his decisions.

When you prepare for a season of polo the money spent and the time taken is not just for one game. Hopefully, there will be many more and from the majority you will have enormous fun. If one game goes wrong through the actions of the umpire, a team mate, an opponent or yourself there is always another day.

CONCLUSION

Whether umpiring or playing, why not always be outside your pony in order to chase a correct position and not the ball? Thereby, you can share with many others the best part and total fun of playing the first and the greatest team sport that was given to the world.

If through polo you wish to meet many different people and nationalities you can travel outside your country to play in other parts of the world. If you maintain all-round vision throughout you will be able to adjust to the different interpretations of the rules and customs you will meet.

Chapter 22

THE FIFTEEN POINTS REVISED

TACTICS

The mnemonic LATET is a useful way to remember the five points of tactics which are given on page 15. LATET stands for:

Look
Adjust
Team
Engage
Turn

Look

This is explained under *All-round vision* on page 15. It is the basis of polo tactics, and all polo players, whether of low or high handicap, should continually seek to improve their application of it. Every sport has the requirement to see what is happening, but in polo, where eight players on ponies move extremely fast, it is vitally important. A good player who watches the other seven all the time will anticipate far better than a weaker opponent who does not. It is similar to driving a car in heavy traffic, when it is essential to see in front and behind in order not to be surprised by other vehicles, people, animals or unexpected obstacles. However, with a mirror for assistance there is no necessity to turn the body.

In polo, which is the part of the body that can help the most for turning and looking behind? The head or neck is the normal spontaneous answer, but this is wrong. Try the feet, at the other end of the body. When the feet turn they will rotate the lower leg and the knees, which twist the thighs and hips, allowing an effortless movement by the shoulders, neck and head. By practising this frequently you will help your striking technique, where the use of all these sections of the body are equally important. You could say "look with your feet".

How can you make yourself look around more? By being consistently watched and graded by another person. He or she could be an official coach, another player, family, friend or groom. Also by using self-discipline during stick and ball practice, you could make yourself look around between every shot. Even better, force yourself to talk aloud by saying "look around, look around" while practising and playing until you have trained the subconscious to take over and do it for you.

Adjust

A slight or large adjustment should be made constructively (as stated on page 15) to everything that takes place on a polo field. On such a large field it is often necessary to make a major change in direction and speed. However, sometimes a brilliant minor adjustment will win a polo match. Again, there is a similarity to driving a car, because this requires endless adjustments, large and small, to all that happens on the road. Much of this is done in anticipation of what is expected to take place.

In polo, as in life, it is mistakes which necessitate the majority of adjustments. These can be made by you, your pony, your team, the opponents or even the ball when it bounces falsely. Mistakes may not matter too much but slow or poor adjustments to them can be disastrous. In fact, if you and your team can react to your mistake quicker than the opposition it may be fortuitous.

Brilliant play by friend or foe can produce surprises which must be adjusted to. Some situations can be changed drastically by bad umpiring, especially when an obvious foul is not called. Uttering swear words will not help because this will delay the adjustment required, which will probably be a violent change in direction.

Often the simplest and most effective way of retrieving an ugly situation is to move laterally, in order to save petrol. A car driver who accelerates and brakes more than is necessary will quickly have an empty petrol tank. How much time do you have before the tank of a polo pony runs out? Seven and a half minutes, if the pony is not asked for too much exertion early on. Speed can be reduced by cutting corners, and braking minimised by sometimes going wider than the direct route. Doing this will give your pony a much easier time and help you to keep cool. The riding school exercises which I devised to help you understand and apply lateral adjustment are described and explained on pages 28, 46 and 64.

How does a player know if he is adjusting correctly and quickly enough during polo matches? "By the results", you might reply. But it is possible to win playing badly, and to lose playing well, besides the fact, which too many people forget, that you can only play as well as you are allowed to. The answer can be supplied by an experienced coach who has the time to observe constructively. In fact it is important to be the recipient of frequent assessments if you want to give a consistently good performance.

Team

The team which is best at filling all four positions consistently is most likely to win. To achieve this all team members must always know where the other three are. To add to what is written on page 15 under the heading *Four positions* a team should continually have two players either side of the barrier, see page 58. By looking and adjusting correctly, as already described, it should be simple to do this.

The ball-chaser looks for the ball first, the nearest opponent second, while expecting the other three in his team to watch and admire him. This is totally wrong; he should reverse the process to make the ball chase him. To do this he needs to discipline his subconscious by frequently asking himself "Where are my team members, especially my No.3; where are all four opponents, in particular the one at present relative to me; and now is the ball chasing me?" This extra emphasis on watching your own No.3 is enormously valuable because it enables you to work closely with your best player while also absorbing some of his superior anticipation.

What is the correct distance between players? It depends on the standard of polo and the striking ability of the individual players. A perfect team, when anticipating a pass from the No.4, should position itself so that a weak shot will reach No.3, an average hit will find No.2

and the best strike could go as far as No.1. By practising together without opposition, doing the exercises which are given in this book, a team can perfect this.

In many teams No.2 is too often in 1½ and is therefore too far from the barrier, with the result that No.1 receives few passes and if the game suddenly changes to defence there is poor marking. It has to be more healthy when No.3 can reach No.1 with his average shot and No.2 with a weak delivery or a deliberate short accurate pass. This formula will increase the depth of the attack and encourage the better midfield players to include their No.1 and No.4 in the proceedings. Otherwise incorrect distances between players on such a large field will allow too much selfish play and the team will then lose the services of at least one if not two members. This unfortunate situation can be further exacerbated by too much use of those dreaded words "leave it". In general, two thirds of "leave its" are wrong for three reasons:

1. Depth in attack is decreased.
2. Defence is weakened, if suddenly required to act.
3. The team dimension is diluted.

To bring about full team involvement will require considerable discipline which can only be imposed by a competent coach. His presence is the best way to produce effective team cohesion and the fastest possible improvement for each individual player.

Engage

This is the hardest part of the game of polo for a beginner to understand and apply correctly. It does, in fact, demonstrate three different ways in which polo is unique amongst all other sports:

1. The path of the ball is always relevant to the rules.
2. Without relation to the ball, players can obstruct each other.
3. The difference in standard of those participating can be enormous. A beginner can play against an international.

The combination of these above three points

provides great scope for one player to make a fool of another, especially when competing for the ball. This is because the weaker player normally cannot apply what is explained on page 15 under *Early closing* and hence the stronger one on almost every occasion will win the engagement (the ride-off) or will make the former commit a foul.

The well known polo cry "Man first, ball second" seems to be obeyed only by the better players. The remainder are denied the glorious enjoyment of physically controlling an opponent when far away from the ball. This presumes that such an action cannot be deemed dangerous. You are more likely to cause an accident by going direct to the ball or by making contact near it than if you engage far away from it, as only permitted in polo. Also, the weaker player, if he stays in contact with a stronger opponent for most of the time, could find that he is always in the correct spot and is frequently taken to where the ball is about to arrive. However, it is very important to separate and differentiate between the following two situations: approaching the ball alone without interference from opponents, and competing against an opponent for the ball.

1. There are four different ways to approach the ball if it appears that no one is behind you and there are no opponents to compete with for the ball.
    a. By going the shortest way directly to the ball.
    b. Making a curved approach in order to hit straight at goal or whatever is the target, possibly crossing the line while doing so.
    c. Taking a short cut to the ball by joining the line half way between the closest point on that line and the ball.
    d. By going to the closest point on the line in order to approach exactly on the line. This is the only guaranteed way to be correct and not foul. By approaching as described in a, b or c there is a risk that a high calibre opponent will appear from nowhere to claim a foul.

2. There are three different ways in which an opponent might compete with you for the

ball and for each one there is a solution applicable to the situation.
    a. Your opponent is behind you and already on the line.
        Solution—Look behind and, as quickly as possible, engage, using a safe angle to win a ride-off. Then stay in contact with your opponent until you have hit the ball.
    b. Your opponent is in front of you and on the other side of the line.
        Solution—Rapidly cross the line, looking only at your opponent (not the ball) and attempt to win the ride-off with a safe engagement. Although your opponent starts with an advantage this action could surprise him. If successful, look behind to check that no one is there to claim the line (the right of way). If not, bring your opponent with you to the line before striking the ball. If someone is now behind you on the line, do not foul him by hitting the ball unless you are confident that the opponent alongside you will be blamed for pushing you across the line.
    c. Your opponent is in front of you but farther away from the line.
        Solution—Rapidly change direction to move towards your opponent, looking only at him (not the ball), to use surprise against his advantage in an attempt to win the ride-off with a safe engagement. If successful and no one is on the line behind you, bring your opponent with you before hitting the ball. Otherwise behave as described above in para 2b.

Whenever approaching the ball, the priority is to look in order to assess the situation correctly and then apply the necessary solution. A sideline coach could assist considerably with constructive criticism on the application of the above solutions with comments made between chukkas and after matches. Of course there is a bonus from winning ride-offs when on the offside of an opponent in order to strike with your strongest shot.

As described in para 2b above, it may be necessary to cross the line before engaging. It is perfectly legal to do so if an opponent is not on the line. This highlights a fallacy that a player may never cross the line of the ball. The rules state that a player may not cross another player who is on the line of the ball.

To sum up, here is a suggested "words and action" process to be used as a control over the normal subconscious reflexes which can mislead inexperienced players badly.

"Where is the line of the ball?"

Start to move towards the nearest point of the line.

"Look for trouble (an opponent close by)."

If an opponent appears rapidly, divert to engage him.

This should help to overcome the desire to ball-chase instead of controlling the opposition and to counter the influence of other sports in which an opponent may only be engaged while he is playing the ball. Such discipline will be augmented by comments from the coach.

Turn

The importance of turning before the play does, and how the other component parts of LATET can assist this to happen, are covered on page 15. The last member of a relay team is in a similar situation to a polo player who has accomplished the first four parts of LATET and then is required to turn. The last relay runner cannot win if the other team members have given a poor performance. Equally if he is off form the efforts of the others will have been wasted. If the polo player turns at the right time the whole LATET formula is successfully completed, but if he turns late the other four component parts will have been wasted.

Too many polo players consistently turn late

because they chase and watch the ball to the exclusion of applying LATET. The turn from defence to attack can be made at four different times:

1. Correctly before the backhand is struck.
2. One move late after the backhand has been struck.
3. Two moves late after the ball has travelled some distance.
4. Three moves late after the striker of the backhand has turned to follow the ball.

The majority of polo players do the third one, and therefore move into all attacks two moves behind the game. This enormous gap between right and wrong will never be redressed until sideline coaching becomes a regular feature in polo. It is especially relevant when defence turns to attack because the only way to defeat an opposition with a strong defence is to be a move ahead of it. To turn early from attack to defence can also be vitally important but the principle is not so dogmatic because there are variations in its application. For example, in front of the barrier it may be preferable if the forwards try to depreciate the opponent's backhand by harassing, impeding and blocking the shot before they turn. Also, behind the barrier, using good anticipation, No.3 and No.4 may well stop before the backhand has been struck in order to meet the ball without turning or to join the line before anyone else.

It is negative and wrong to argue that a late turn is justified in expectation of a missed backhand. If the distances between players are correctly applied as suggested under the heading *Team* one of them should be capable of quickly adjusting to regain possession of the ball after a backhand is missed. It is vital to prevent the following thought process from taking place: "Will he miss? He has hit, but will the ball reach me? Oh yes, the ball has gone past me so now I must turn" (two moves too late). The subconscious must therefore be tightly controlled and this can be helped by carrying out exercises which train players to turn before backhands are struck. These should include the practice of verbalising turning while actually doing it. This must be repeated, even during matches, until it is clear that the early turn has become an automatic action. If a coach is always present to criticise this dimension, the process of improvement will be speeded up and the possibility of returning to the bad habit of making late turns will be reduced.

The standard of polo in any club would be raised dramatically if there was a period of coaching which concentrated on the skills of turning early. This would also increase the ability of all players to apply the other four parts of LATET.

RIDING

I have taught many weak riders to play polo since this book was first published. After three or four sessions of riding exercises the improvement in their horsemanship has, normally, been unbelievable both to themselves and observers. This is because, before the instruction began, they had little or no comprehension of my riding principles, and after being forced to apply them for those few concentrated periods they found that, instead of taking the rider around the field, the pony preferred to follow the rider. I have added new exercises and competitions to the riding programme but still teach the same five principles, with a greater depth of explanation than there is on pages 16, 17 and 18.

Outside the pony

There is little to add to what is written on pages 15 and 16 but it may be interesting to examine the dimension that a pony is a non-predator, hence the eyes are on the side of the head instead of the front as in the case of the predator. The pony can, therefore, see all around without difficulty, and, as a wild animal in his natural habitat, this all-around vision provides him with an early warning of the presence of the distrusted predator. Once a pony is broken, backed and well trained, he will learn to trust a good rider even though that person has the predator's frontal eyes. This confidence in the rider will be increased further if the eyes of man and pony never meet; both sets of eyes should be focused on the same thing, thereby establishing perfect communication. A weak rider will not only feel wrong when on top of a

pony but will also impart a further loss of confidence whenever their eyes meet because, suddenly, the rider becomes the predator who threatens the pony by looking at him instead of with him.

The ability to achieve the tactical requirement to look will help greatly in being outside the pony, and the constant turning of the lower limbs, especially the feet, will assist in keeping the eyes separated, i.e. "look with your feet".

Weight on saddle front

The main reasons for using the fork position on the front of the saddle are given on page 16. Besides these the fork position will also assist a rider to look around better, to have more effective grip with the legs and to be gentler with the hands on the reins. There is also an added advantage for the striking technique because from the front of the saddle it is easier to hit the ball early which is so important for the majority of the shots.

Look and go

To clarify this heading on page 16 even further, I should point out that the aim is to make the pony follow the rider instead of the other way round. The pony must also change direction at the required moment and not when he wants to; he should not turn when the rider looks, but later at the precise time that the neck rein is applied and the rider's weight is projected in the relevant direction. During the turn the rider ought not to see his pony, and that includes the head of the pony. This will prevent the possibility of the pony suddenly regarding the rider as a predator instead of a person with whom he should cooperate. Anything which might confuse the pony could make him reluctant to change direction rapidly and then valuable time will be lost.

Minimum use of hands

If the pony is always willing to follow the rider any contact through the reins on the mouth must be minimised. Also frequent use of lateral adjustment will necessitate much neck reining and prevent the rider from pulling on the pony's mouth, which could be called braking. Another way to reduce the amount of braking is for the rider to look back before halting. Here again it is the combination of the eyes of both rider and pony that is so effective that a long, loose rein need seldom be tightened by a good, sympathetic rider on a well-trained pony.

Strong legs

The rider must realise that the legs can help a horse as well as punish him. The legs should give the final confirmation of what the eyes and projected weight have already told the pony. To move forward, turn or stop, a similar squeeze of the legs in the direction in which the rider is looking will impart the necessary impulsion. If the pony does not react immediately, however, a well-executed kick behind the girth can impose obedience. However, weak riders should be careful not to kick without realising it because they are apt to do this when their toes hang down and out. Lastly, a pony that does not oblige when asked to stop can be controlled by an extra squeeze of the legs without any kick, which will lift up his front and help him to throw all his weight backwards. This action is improved further if both pony and rider look back together.

STRIKING

The approach

Placing the pony to the ball and self-briefing. By first looking to see exactly where the ball should go, a polo player is briefing himself to focus directly at the spot on the ball which has to be struck. This action will assist him a great deal to place the pony early and correctly to the ball, using the two clocks which are shown on page 32. During the approach for a backhand, an arc must be made to provide scope for the polo mallet to travel through a full circle at the required angle without hitting the head or tail of the pony.

The preparation

Warming up and selecting the stick and hand position. The right hand and its fingers require a constant supply of blood in order to maintain total control of a polo mallet. This is best achieved by frequently revolving the mallet through 360 degrees. The thumb and index finger allow the mallet to fall and then flick it back into an upright position. With practice this should become an effortless action. I call it warming up, which can either be done clockwise or anti-clockwise. Even when far away from the ball, warm-ups will enable a player to be able to strike at a second's notice. When approaching the ball, ideally one warm up should be done just before the swing starts. The better players can afford to incorporate the warm up with the swing, but the beginner needs more time to construct his shot and must warm up earlier in order to start the swing from the correct stick and hand position as described in Chapters 5, 8, 11 and 14.

The swing

Using the shoulders to set the pendulum. The feet, thighs, and hips should rotate under the shoulders when they turn as described on page 18. At the same time the right hand makes the preliminary swing so that a straight line is formed between the hand, the spot and the target. For the majority of shots (not all) the above action supports the placing of the mallet head in the direction of the target. Now the mallet head is correctly set as a pendulum, which must not be allowed to waver.

The contact

The slow hand to the sweet spot. The centre of the mallet head is the extension of the right hand. It is much easier to aim at the spot on the ball with the right hand than with the mallet head. The downward movement of the hand at the selected spot should be executed very slowly. Only then will the pendulum operate correctly because now the mallet head has time to complete the desired perfect circle and thus reach the ball ahead of the hand. This will maximise the velocity of the mallet head without using arm strength, but if the hand moves too fast the mallet head will be forced to take a short cut across the circle and will not reach the ball ahead of the hand, thus preventing the mallet head from accelerating sufficiently, and encouraging the use of arm strength. All that is said on page 18 still applies, but while aiming for the spot "slow hand" can be used as the alternative operative words.

The follow through

The completion of the shot. Consistent accuracy and length can only be achieved by applying the follow through as described on page 18, but this is not sufficient to exert enough control on the mallet head, which has accelerated rapidly en route to the ball. Therefore, after contact, and when the whole mallet is at full stretch in the direction of the target, the hand should once again allow the mallet to revolve through 360 degrees. This will dissipate the power which has been gathered by the mallet head and at the same time prevent a lateral deviation from accuracy.

Chapter 23

TACTICS "G"

THE ROPE

If LATET is diligently applied by all four members of a polo team it will be simple for them to operate the rope formation as explained on pages 107, 108 and 109. Some people think the rope is for tying people together. On the contrary, the object is to check the herd instinct and prevent ball-chasers from charging into each other. If the rope is hypothetically kept taut at all times the objective will be achieved and the correct distance between each player will be maintained throughout fluid attacks.

Since this book was first published I have instructed many people in a variety of countries and often watched the best players in the world compete against each other. This experience has shown me that the rope concept is not only correct but that it is the basis of all tactics in polo. Once a beginner understands the rope principle he should find that it is relatively simple to be in or near the correct position for most of the time. The game will also appear to be less complicated and he should begin to contribute constructively to the tactics of his team.

From every set piece situation the rope formation should be in place quickly, and after moments of fluid play it should be re-established immediately. When there is a throw in, a hit in or a hit from the spot which successfully starts an attack the rope ought to be visible after a maximum of two hits. In defence the rope is the only way to contain the opposition who keep possession of the ball long enough to threaten the goal.

On page 107 the description of the rope exercise is that each player will in turn have a straight shot at goal whether or not the previous hit was accurate. This of course precludes the existence of opposition who, when present, can easily be fouled by anyone leaving the line to aim at the goal. In fact it is important to realise that only the next striker need be on the present line of the ball while the other three in his team should be anticipating the line which that striker will create. However if the ball does run down the anticipated line and in the direction of the goal the next striker will legally have a straight shot at goal, but when there is inaccuracy, which often happens, the next striker must hit an angled shot at goal and then remain on the line until well after the shot is completed in order not to foul an opponent who is behind him. Only if there is no one behind can a striker adjust his approach for a straight shot at goal.

On page 106 the method of using a mini ground (60 yards long) to play and practice on foot is discussed and mini sticks with a soft ball are recommended. Since then I have found that much time is saved if mini sticks are dispensed with and a polo ball is thrown from player to player instead. People can throw very accurately most of the time and seldom is anyone struck by the ball, which can still run down a line before being picked up.

To understand and utilise fully all the ramifications and benefits of the rope, whether you are a beginner or not, I do suggest that you humble yourself at least once by walking with three others holding a rope while doing the exercise sequence as suggested. A few variations of the route to goal should highlight all the lessons that can be learnt. Do not be confused by the order of hitting being Nos.4, 3, 2, 1. In a practice chukka or a polo match a strong hit by No.4 could be received by No.2 or even No.1, but the purpose of this exercise is that Nos.2 and 1 are unable to take the second shot, and that No.1 is similarly prevented from taking the third shot but is able to hit the fourth. In this way the ball has to be shared, while the problem of maintaining a taut rope when not hitting the ball is encountered, and, if achieved, demonstrates the importance of doing so with great clarity.

The next stage is to repeat the exercise on foot without holding the rope. To make this fully effective a coach should watch, or even take part, so that without the restraint of a rope the maintenance of correct distances and the anticipation of the next line is forced upon you and, hopefully, stored in your subconscious. It will also demonstrate the difference in

Tactics "G"

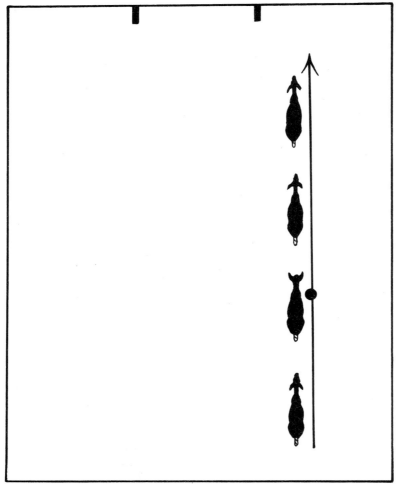

Incorrect

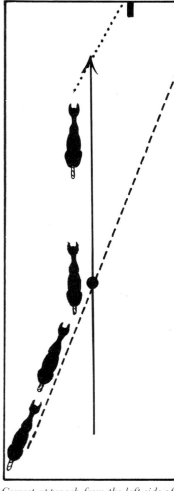

Correct approach from the left side of

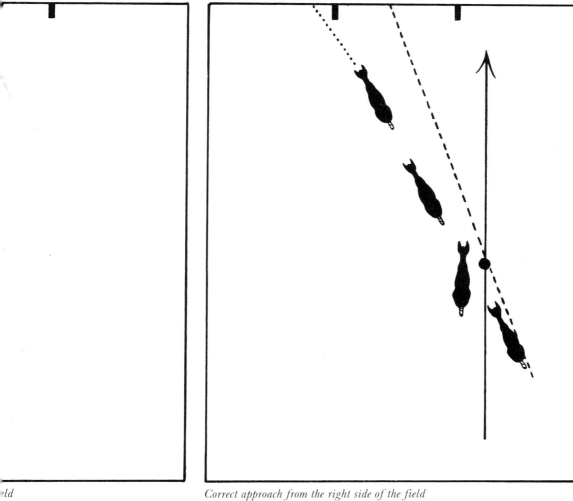

Correct approach from the right side of the field

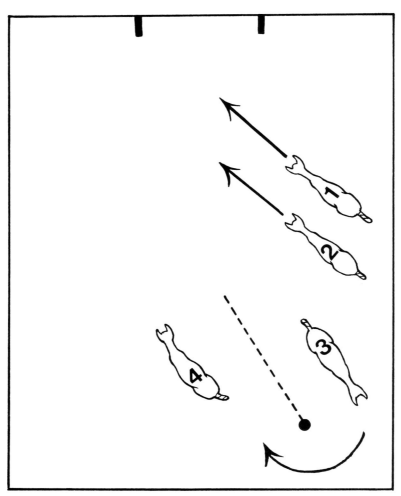

Stage One of the reverse rope

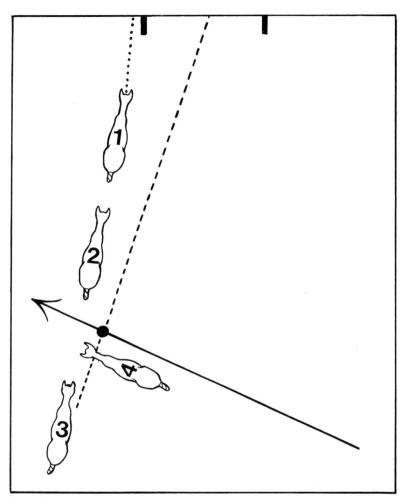

Stage Two of the reverse rope

behaviour of the three players who are not about to hit the ball according to whether they are in front of or behind the ball, although all are seeking the line expected from the next shot. Those in front must position themselves between the left-hand goal post and the next striker, ready to join the new line as it runs past them. Those behind should swing left or right to be exactly on the line of the next shot before the strike is even made. This can put the whole team one or two moves ahead of the opposition. For example, if the above is carried out correctly, but No.2, although hitting accurately, does not send the ball far enough to reach No.1 and then moves in front of the ball, No.3, who joined the existing line so early, will have gained a big advantage for taking the next shot before any opponent. Of course, someone will say that if No.2 misses his first shot completely, No.3 then will not be on the existing line. However, in this situation, No.3 could possibly win a ride-off against an opponent who claims the line from behind him. Another advantage is that, should an opponent successfully ride-off No.2 and then angle a backhand to one side, No.3 may then have an easy meet without fouling.

Once the stick and ball phase arrives, the above rope exercise should be repeated on a full-size polo field. I have never had the courage to connect mounted players with a rope; however, a cry of "tighten the rope" does make people check their positioning, which effectively controls the herd and ball-chasing instinct of anyone who has done the exercise on foot with a rope. To start, the ball is placed on one goal line with the No.3 alongside it, Nos.1 and 2 in front of it and No.4 behind it. For beginners the No.1 should not be further away than the 30 yard line with No.2 no more than 15 yards into the field while No.4 is 15 yards behind the ball. For better players No.1 could move to the 60 yard line, No.2 to the 30 yard line and No.4 can withdraw further behind the ball. The aim is that it is easy for each striker to reach the player in front of him while the distances between team members remains constant from one end of the field to the other.

If there is more than one team practicing the rope drill on ponies at the same time, an impor-

tant degree of pressure can be generated by having a race. A coach should act as referee to supervise fair play and see that no one hits twice in succession and that all four have hit the ball before it reaches the far goal. Therefore if No.1 does not reach the goal with the fourth shot, No.4 should take the fifth and the sequence starts again. Afterwards the coach can criticise the performance, including distances and positioning for the line before the ball is hit. Besides being enjoyable the rope race is a way of producing conditions similar to a polo match. There is real pressure and a lot of scope for making mistakes which must be adjusted to, and can draw a helpful criticism from the sideline.

THE REVERSE ROPE

In a good team, if an angled pass from one player reaches another the remaining two team members should adjust laterally to conform and establish a new rope formation. When achieved, this emphasises the effectiveness of team play, creates surprise, and produces a manoeuvre which the opposition will find difficult to contain. There are many different ways in which the above tactic can be done but I recommend that players learn the concept by practising as a team the drill called the reverse rope. This begins with an interchange between No.3 and No.4 which ensures that No.4 is involved and the ramifications of his participation in attack are realised by all.

This exercise demonstrates how quickly defence can be converted into attack. It starts with everyone in defence facing the backline in the normal team order on the rope. The ball is between Nos.3 and 4 and the first shot, a backhand, is hit by No.3, who either opens or tails the ball depending on the direction in which No.4 turns.

"When No.3 takes a backhand he becomes No.4" says Gonzalo Pieres, the best player in the world during the last decade. In this exercise the second shot, a forehand, is hit by No.4, who should turn to become No.3 before the backhand has been struck. Nos.1 and 2 must anticipate what is happening and adjust to be in front of No.4 and to be heading for the left goal post before the second shot is struck. Then No.2 takes the third hit and No.1 the fourth while obeying all the rules for the rope formation. If No.1 does not reach the goal with his shot, then No.3 must designate who takes the succeeding strikes with the objective that there is equal involvement by all; and he must try to ensure that nobody hits the ball twice in succession.

Many teams that I have watched seldom execute this clever tactic because the No.3 prefers to turn with the ball instead of distributing it with an intelligent backhander. Also No.4s who can only think about defence miss many opportunities to initiate this tactic. Any team which frequently practices the reverse rope as an exercise will find that it is easy to introduce it in a match. I include it in my mini field sessions on foot and then in the periods of stick and ball. Again, there is scope for races if there is more than one team present. Whether racing or not it is preferable to be watched by a coach, who can criticise distances and other important details besides adjudicating if required.

In chukkas and matches it will depend on the length of No.3's backhand as to who takes the second shot but ideally No.4 becomes No.3 regardless of whether he hits or not. In many situations a short and wide backhand which is received by No.4 will be the most effective way to unhinge the marking of the opposition. Then if Nos.1 and 2 form the rope in front of No.4, they should have a good chance of carrying out a sequence of passes without much interference from the opposition. The main secret for success is for all three players to turn before No.3 hits the backhand and then maintain their distances to keep possession of the ball.

If the opponents suddenly regain the ball and the No.4 finds that he is in front of the ball, then, in order to defend, he must immediately re-establish his position behind the ball. This has to be an automatic action, designated as part of No.4's job, otherwise he cannot be allowed to join the attacks too often. He will then probably have to make a defensive play, but might again have an opportunity to initiate another reverse rope if he sees his No.3 taking a backhand.

As stated above, the No.4 in a match should initiate the reverse rope by turning left or right early enough to let No.3 strike a suitable backhand pass. It is also feasible for No.3 to call to his No.4 to turn left or right but the latter may not have enough time to effect the required interchange. Another variation is that No.4 turns so early and moves so fast that he moves into No.2 or even reaches No.1 on the rope. In either case the rest of the team must adjust appropriately and hold the rope together. In fact LATET should be applied throughout to make this tactic successful, and in between matches an input from a coach will help to rectify any mistakes being made.

THE THROW-IN

The game of polo can be opened out quickly if teams have a good throw-in drill. This is already explained on page 57, but, in order to achieve it, emphasis must be placed on the fact that all the team during a throw-in are standing together and alongside the No.3. Thus, it is very important that Nos.1 and 4 move quickly, because the rope formation will not be established until No.1 has moved upfield through two positions to be an instant link to goal while No.4 has retreated the opposite way to shut the back door. Even if the opposition gain initial possession of the ball, No.1 must not turn to defence until it is blatantly clear that their attack is continuing successfully. The reason is that one good backhand from any team member would be wasted if No.1 was moving in defence instead of positioning himself in anticipation of receiving the pass.

Similarly, No.4 should not be misled into following an attack by his team from the throw-in until it is beyond all doubt that the attack will succeed. Again, one backhand, this time from an opponent, would cause problems if it went through an open back door and the opposing No.1 was able to head for goal without restraint.

The No.1s are always in danger of becoming involved in a useless battle against each other at the throw-in. Despite having the intention of avoiding each other, a blockage may occur if they both try to do the same thing. Although far-fetched it is reasonable for the No.1s to agree beforehand who will go in front and who will pass behind the other at all the throw-ins. For beginners this is better than being cursed by other players.

If the ball is thrown all the way through the line up, No.4 may head an attack (see page 58), but he must be careful not to commit a foul against the opposing No.3 who may have turned round in the line up to follow the ball. Also he should avoid interfering with his own No.3 who may have been the first to turn in the line up to claim the line and should be given preference. In fact in this situation No.4 could initiate the reverse rope.

THE HIT-IN

A suggested system for the hit-in using a diamond formation is described on page 42. I hasten to add that there are many other ways and formations for executing the hit-in successfully; they all require conscientious application of LATET throughout and all should terminate with the team on the rope. Remember that one mistake could give a goal away whereas a well-executed drill can produce a score at the far end of the field.

If you watch some bad polo teams you will notice that while No.4 or maybe No.3 takes the hit-in the other three players stand still, waiting to see where the ball will go; they then have to improvise and move hastily to where the action is. It would be far better if the opposition have to hurry to counter the unexpected while the team hitting-in calmly carry out a preplanned strategy.

Ideally the ball from any hit-in should, indirectly or even directly, reach No.1 as quickly as possible. The various ways in which this can be achieved should be rehearsed regularly and in polo matches there will be an advantage of surprise if the opposition never know which one to expect. Each hit-in drill can itself be varied but for consistent effective results coordination from a coach is needed. His constructive comments during practice, between chukkas and after matches will help enormously.

The crushed diamond can be very efficient because the opponents have to spread wide to cover all the possible alternatives thereby enabling the team hitting-in to employ lateral

adjustment freely in order to establish a rope after only two strikes. But none of the alternatives can be executed successfully if anyone makes a mistake or is casual with his part of the drill. To minimise such problems and to achieve ongoing drill improvement during a season, coach control will be vital. The following mistakes are those which could cause the problems, but they ought to be easy to correct if observed from the sideline:

1. No.2 starts from a position too far upfield or infield with the result that the ball either does not reach him or when it does arrive he is almost static.
2. No.2 has mobility but turns upfield too soon before the ball can reach him.
3. No.1 stays in the midfield too long or moves too far upfield and is unable to receive an average length pass.
4. No.4, when taking the hit, starts so close to the ball that this prevents the remainder of the team from gathering the necessary speed to avoid being marked.
5. No.4, when not expected, first taps the ball and then slowly makes the second hit thus allowing the opponents to engage the other three team members before the ball reaches them.
6. No.4 or No.3 hits in too straight or inaccurately, giving the ball away to the opposition.
7. No.3 positions wrongly and obstructs the mobility of the hit-in.

FACING THE HIT-IN

Two systems for opposing the hit-in are suggested on pages 59–63 and these are explained in detail with diagrams. They are "the box" and a "modified box" which provides increased opportunities for meeting the ball. There are other alternatives which include the simple system of marking one on one. This is done in two ways:

1. No.1 against opponent No.4, No.2 against No.3, No.3 against No.2, and No.4 against No.1.
2. No.1 against opponent No.4, No.2 against No.2, No.3 against No.3, and No.4 against No.1.

These systems are mainly defensive and can be very effective for preventing the opponents' hit-in from mounting a successful attack, but the chances of making an immediate counterattack are limited compared to "the box" system.

Depending on the opponents' hit-in drill, to face it, a different formation could be used for each match. It is easier to do this if the opposition have been watched in previous matches, and, ideally, this is the task of a coach. He could also be helpful in pinpointing, during practices and matches, if and why the team does fail to control the opponents when they hit-in. The following are mistakes he might observe and correct:

1. No.1 being drawn to the area of the ball instead of remaining correctly positioned to receive a pass or mark the last opponent.
2. No.2 chasing the ball regardless of where it lands.
3. No.3 using his speed to the disadvantage of his team by making a backhand too quickly without first engaging an opponent so that the ball is given away to the opposition although it was intercepted.
4. No.4 staying static, watching others too long instead of ensuring that he shuts the back door.

THE RIDE-OFF

Two basic requirements to win a ride-off are given on page 57. Since writing them, experience has shown that there are five parts which should be studied and applied. The ride-off is the best way to gain possession of the ball. By doing so, not only does a player have the next strike, but also an opponent under his control cannot intercept his hit by anticipating where he will send the ball. Also, the opponent is unable to collect the ball after a miss.

A ride-off should be a positive engagement, as defined under LATET, because it should safely take over the right of way from an opponent without fouling him. A player is not allowed to wait on the line of the ball for an opponent to arrive but can push him off that line in order to take control of what I call the "main road" to the ball. It is even better if the opponent can be

firmly engaged before the ball arrives or a long way before reaching it. Then the player should be able to maintain total control while allowing the opponent to push him to the line (road) before the ball is reached.

To win a ride-off it is vital to concentrate more on the opponent than the ball because he wants to hit the ball and will take you to it. However, many things can go wrong with a ride-off because good timing is necessary and there are tricks which are often played to upset it. The high-handicap players are expert at these tricks, and because people of such varying standards meet on the playing field (a trait unique to polo), it is important to learn and apply the correct technique, but this is difficult without good coaching that covers all five parts.

1. *Positioning* The best place to be is in front of any opponent before trying to engage him. If an adversary is chasing the ball without looking around it is easy to come from behind him, engage, and win a ride-off, but if he sees the threat coming it will be very difficult. Therefore, if possible, always adjust to be ahead before engaging in a ride-off.
2. *Speed* This must be increased or slowed down to the same speed of the victim. The most dangerous dimension of polo is when ponies travelling at very different velocities make physical contact. If one is moving much faster or much slower than the other there is certain to be a foul if not an accident. If the change of speed cannot be effected it is better to try to hook or allow the opponent one more shot before engaging him. Changing speed correctly is vital.
3. *Angle* The correct angle of engagement depends on the speed. When moving fast, a wide angle is dangerous and a narrow one is sufficient to win, but, when going slowly a wide angle is not only safe but also necessary to win. Hence, once in front and moving at the ideal speed, the appropriate angle must be selected.
4. *Look* To carry out the above three points correctly a player must look very carefully at the victim and ensure that no third party is

involved. Then, at the moment of engaging, watch for clever tricks; these can only be countered by a direct focus on the eyes of the opponent. Look at his eyes.

5. *Retaliation* Just when a ride-off seems to be won against a good player, he will try to reverse the situation. To counter this, retaliate by giving him an extra push away from the line of the ball before hitting the ball.

To sum up the art of riding-off: it is important to position in front, change to the correct speed, select a safe and effective angle, look at the eyes of the opponent and retaliate first.

Chapter 24

POLO RIDING "F"

CRITIQUE OF THE RIDING

By participating in the riding school drills and exercises described in Chapters 4, 7, 10 and 13 weak riders will improve enormously, and the more experienced will learn to use tips which previously may not have occurred to them. Many players who have developed a good tactical sense and have learnt to strike the ball well cannot, in a match, employ these skills, because they lack sufficient pony control. Others will never develop these skills until their riding proficiency improves enough to enable them to move about the polo field correctly and accurately in relation to the rest of their team.

Overcoming weaknesses and developing strengths could be assisted by someone watching from the sideline who can give helpful advice. Players can also coach themselves through the eyes of another person whom they request to observe specific points, but an experienced coach criticising the important riding skills regularly is the best solution. Whatever the arrangement, the relevant riding points can be covered by the following list of questions:

1. How often do you look at the pony?
2. Do you jerk the mouth of the pony too much?
3. Are your reins too short?
4. Do you slip to the back of the saddle?
5. Do you turn without first looking?
6. Do you stop without looking back?
7. Are you using your whip too little or too much?
9. Are your legs assisting correctly the pony to both accelerate and stop?
9. Do you kick the pony unintentionally?
10. Do you turn faster or slower than an opponent alongside you?
11. Do you accelerate slower than the average opponent?

The answers to the above questions plus constructive comments from a coach or helper should make any polo player aware of his riding faults. Hopefully, over a period of time, the answers will demonstrate an improvement in riding skills. If not there are drills and remedies which could be done on non-polo days or even immediately before playing. Unless there is a skilled trainer available, the requirement to school polo ponies between polo days could be combined with these drills. To explain how this schooling might be done the numbering used for the above questions is repeated to give the relevant remedies on the presumption that an improvement is needed.

1. Design a programme which helps you acquire the skill of being outside the pony. This should include figures of eight, circles, turns, and stops and must be completed without ever seeing the pony. Throughout the movements, exaggerate the action of looking around and away from the pony.
2. While doing the programme in 1 above, experiment with ways to reduce contact on the mouth of the pony as follows:
   a. Exaggerate the use of neck reining and looking back to stop with a long rein.
   b. Place one finger of your left hand under the martingale strap and try to take weight on this finger before the reins.
   c. At times, quietly apply two hands on the reins, especially when stopping.
3. To practise riding with longer reins, touch your stomach frequently with your left hand; there should be no contact on the pony's mouth.
4. To counter slipping back in the saddle, use the martingale strap to pull yourself forward. Then pivot all your body weight on the pommel of the saddle, turning to left and right by rotating feet, thighs and hips.
5. To make you look before turning, select a marker such as a flag, post or tree, then canter past the marker, turn to look at the marker, focusing firmly on it, and, lastly, turn the pony by neck reining while maintaining your focus on the marker. To ensure you do the drill correctly call out the words "look, look" before neck reining to turn. Do this drill to the left and to the right. When

satisfied with the result repeat the drill at increased speed with a view to turning smoothly at the gallop in due course.

6. To help you look back before stopping, use the same marker you used in 5 above. Repeat the drill but instead of neck reining, halt. Brief yourself to look back, focus on the marker while squeezing hard with your legs and, only then, if necessary, quietly and smoothly pull on the reins. After a good result gradually increase the speed, but do not allow the action to become rough.

7. Holding the whip correctly, preventing it from upsetting the pony when not in use, and being able to use the whip effectively when required, needs practice. The whip, held in the left hand, should be touching the outside of the left thigh in order not to flick, or in any way intimidate, the pony. Occasionally a whip drill, without hitting the pony, should be practised: throw the reins from your left to your right hand, then raise your left hand and whip high behind you, drop the whip behind the saddle without touching the pony's flank, retake the reins with your left hand, and, lastly, simulate hitting a ball with your right hand. Perfect the whip drill first at the halt, secondly at the walk, and only then try it when mobile during the programme in 1 above.

8. To strengthen the legs for effective accelerating and stopping requires persistance and patience. By riding regularly, schooling and playing polo often, the legs will gradually become more efficient. For a quicker result you must ride without stirrups (see page 18), or even bareback but, initially, be careful not to overdo this as pulled riding muscles can result. Limit the amount of time without stirrups to a few minutes the first day and then gradually increase as you become stronger. Even then have rest periods when your legs should hang down and be relaxed.

9. To avoid kicking the pony unintentionally, point your toes slightly inwards, towards the pony's mouth. This will prevent your toes pointing down and outwards which makes your heel continually bang or rub against the side of the pony; this happens before riders develop their grip with the legs.

10. If you are turning slower than opponents you should practise the drill (page 64) for the outward turn when riding in pairs in the riding school. This uses the tail trick where precision and patience are vital. You must wait for the tail of the opponent to be opposite the nose of your pony before turning inside him. To do this in a polo match is much harder than in practice. Therefore, when playing, any opportunity to do this trick should be taken for the sake of experience.

11. If you do have problems with accelerating you should design a specific programme. This could include many changes of pace, often stopping, restarting and reining back before restarting. Initially use the whip to show the pony exactly what is required and then gradually limit its use until your legs independently can produce rapid acceleration.

Chapter 25

STRIKING "F"

CRITIQUE OF THE STRIKING TECHNIQUE

What is the most important part of the striking technique? There have been many healthy arguments about this question. In Chapter 22 the five striking points have been revised, but not much has been changed and it is clear that all five points are equally important. If one point is neglected the chance of a good shot is greatly reduced.

Polo players should always be looking for ways to improve their striking technique. Problems need to be identified before they become a bad habit which cannot be corrected. Poor tactical positioning, for example, will be the cause of many shots having to be rushed. Also, weak riding will result in an inability to approach the ball correctly. Otherwise, to locate a fault, a defect in one or more of the five points of striking will have to be searched for.

Such an examination of the five points, the approach, preparation, swing, contact, and follow through, should happen firstly during stick and ball and secondly in a polo match. It will show whether there is a basic fault in technique or if problems only surface under pressure. Many people do not take into account what a difference pressure will make.

An experienced coach should be able to diagnose the cause of bad technique and quickly recognise the signs of pressure. However, if a coach cannot be obtained, assess yourself with the help of a willing observer. Get him to watch you play the ten shots covered in Chapters 5, 8, 11 and 14. These are listed below as a reminder:

OFFSIDE FOREHANDS
Straight
Neck
Cut

NEARSIDE FOREHANDS
Straight
Neck
Cut

BACKHANDS
Offside open
Tail
Nearside open
Tail

Then, the observer could make the required assessment by asking you the following questions:

The approach
1. Do you place the pony correctly to the ball?
2. Are you remembering to look at the target before preparing to strike?
3. Is a spot on the ball being selected?

The preparation
4. Do you warm up before hitting?
5. Is the polo mallet carried like a heavy weapon?
6. Do you use the necessary stick and hand position?

The swing
7. Is the mallet head being set as a pendulum?
8. Are you turning your hips and shoulders sufficiently?
9. Does the mallet head fall sideways or backwards?

The contact
10. Are you hitting slowly or too hard?
11. Does your hand seek a spot on the ball?
12. Do you hit early or late?

The follow through
13. Does the mallet head point at the target at the end of each shot?
14. Do you look up too soon?
15. After forehands does the mallet revolve 360 degrees?

It is to be hoped that the answers to the above fifteen questions will only show that one or two problems exist and that, basically, you are doing the right things. To be told that you are doing anything correctly will add to your confidence and all helpful suggestions will increase your proficiency. Stick and ball practice can be used constructively to correct any faults—and to experiment with any ideas given to you during and after polo matches.

The following explanations of what could be wrong and how improvements might be made are numbered to correspond with the fifteen questions your coach or your observer asked you above.

1. If you are placing the pony incorrectly to the ball, it may be because you do it too late and join the line too close to the ball. Either reason can cause you to be laterally either too near or too far from the ball when striking. This in turn can prevent a proper swing which will upset accuracy. For backhands there is an extra dimension required to assist with the angle for opening or tailing; a slight curve in the approach will help keep the pony's head or hindquarters, whichever is relevant, out of the way although care must be taken not to foul. Initially this could be practised without actually hitting a ball.

2. Briefing is incomplete if you do not look at the target before hitting. This should be done as early as possible to enable you to hit slowly. In addition, you are less likely to look up if you know the exact direction of the target. To combat this fault you should practise on a wooden horse or at a slow pace on a pony.

3. The spot on the ball does help accuracy enormously. The earlier you select it the more likely you are to connect with it. Therefore, during the approach you must focus on the spot. If you have difficulty with this try talking about it to yourself while approaching.

4. If you have trouble with warming up you should push yourself to develop the habit of doing so. It is important to keep providing a flow of blood to the right hand. This gives the hand more strength and control and although some economy of effort, so vital for beginners, is lost, the warm-up is even more important. For both forehands and backhands, however, the inexperienced player should try to warm up early enough in order to master the use of a static hand and stick, and thus conserve energy.

5. Lifting a polo mallet before striking the ball does increase the power of the shot but the effort of controlling the weight is very likely to make you hit late unless you are moving very slowly. If this should become a bad habit it must be countered by coaching. The warm-up is a better way to derive extra velocity.

6. Application of the correct stick and hand position provides economy of effort, thus preventing you from carrying a heavy mallet, and helps you not to hit late. Only the better handicap players can afford to miss out this phase by incorporating it in the swing. To prevent problems with this, making full shots without a ball should be practised.

7. The swing must control the mallet head. The stick and hand position will set the pendulum in place, but if this phase is missed out, the swing will do the job. The pendulum is vital for accuracy, hence any problem must be corrected by constant practise.

8. If you are not turning your body to help the swing you will probably use arm strength. If this is a problem, compensate by exaggerating the use of the feet by turning 90 degrees to the left or right during the swing. Try to feel that there is a connection between hand and hip which increases body rotation. For the nearside the body turn is even more vital to make you swing like a tennis player instead of a squash player.

9. It is important that the pendulum swings in a perfect circle to produce accuracy and length. If you find this difficult, prevent the mallet head from falling sideways or backwards by dipping it slightly when swinging, and make a very slow smooth shot.

10. If you normally hit too fast and hard, the cure is to experience the magic of connecting with the ball when hitting very slowly. This will prove to you how the mallet head can accelerate effortlessly to reach the ball in front of, and before, the hand. Saying "slow hand" will help you to control it. It is

The forehand drive — top of the swing. (Photo: Max Whitaker.)

even more important to hit slowly on the nearside in order to obtain length.

11. Remember the hand cannot miss. Thus, if it seeks a spot, the hand will be deadly accurate. Simply imagine your hand actually hitting the ball; it will be easier to apply this if you focus on the spot early.

12. If your contact with the ball is always late, it is almost certainly a fault with your approach and/or the preparation. To combat this problem attempt to strike very early, first at a slow pace, then at gradually increasing speeds.

13. It is wasteful if your striking technique is correct except for the follow through. Poor execution of the follow through can be caused by the body collapsing back into the saddle after contact with the ball, and the polo mallet will therefore fall to one side instead of pointing at the target as the shot finishes. Counteract this by keeping your feet firmly turned sideways until the follow through is complete.

14. Worrying about what will happen to the shot will make you look up too soon. Hitting too hard and too fast will have the same effect. Try curing this problem by picking targets very close to you and concentrating on leaving your head and eyes down for even longer than is necessary.

15. A 360 degree revolution by the mallet at the end of the follow through will prevent any lateral deviation from accuracy. The thumb, index finger and the little finger must be coordinated in order to execute this. Another bonus is that the speed at which the mallet head is travelling will dissipate quickly, allowing the next shot to be made sooner. In addition some extra power will be exerted on the contact between mallet and ball. Keep practising this revolution until it becomes an automatic action.

Chapter 26

TACTICS "H"

THE JOBS OF THE PLAYERS REVISED

In Chapters 3, 6 and 9 the jobs of Nos.1, 2, 3 and 4 were described and discussed in detail. Since writing those descriptions, experience has taught me that it is simpler to give each player one job which is subdivided into four tasks. The headings for these tasks can be easily remembered with the mnemonic PRST:

Position   How to stay correctly positioned in relation to your team.

Responsibility   How to strike the ball for the tactical benefit of your team.

Speed   When to use and maximise velocity.

Turn to Defence   When to act defensively although your team is still in attack.

The Jobs
No.1: Links to goal.
No.2: Links from the barrier to No.1.
No.3: Pivots the team from behind the barrier.
No.4: Shuts the back door.

In sport there are principles about which you cannot be totally dogmatic because there are always exceptions to them. Bearing this in mind the four jobs and PRST could be laid in conjunction with one another as follows:

No.1	*Links to goal*
P	Always use two points of reference, one in front and one behind. In attack—be between the left goal post and the next striker in your team. In defence—be between your team and the last opponent.
R	Keep the ball in play when in possession. In front of the goal, aim at a point in line with the centre of the goal but much closer. On the sideline, link to the goal with a backhand. On opponent's backline, prevent the ball from crossing the line.
S	Give your team velocity in attack in two alternative ways: When in front of the ball—keep the rope taut but do not drop it (by going too far upfield). When in possession of the ball—move as fast as possible.
T	Before the start of an attack by opponents, there could be two alternative situations: The opposing No.4 is near you—engage him as soon as possible The opposing No.4 is far behind you—watch him while maintaining a link with the team.

No.2	*Links from the barrier to No.1*
P	Maintain place in front of and close to the barrier.
R	Hit constructively: To keep the ball in front of the barrier To ensure No.1 frequently receives the ball.
S	Maximise velocity when switching between the two conflicting priorities: Marking the opposing No.3 Receiving passes from own No. 3.
T	When own No.3 crosses the barrier replace and cover him: Primarily to keep the defence secure Secondly to add extra depth to the attack.

No.3	*Pivots the team from behind the barrier*
P	Maintain place behind, and close to the barrier.
R	Distribute the ball over the barrier by: Giving accurate angled passes Crossing barrier only when safe to do so.
S	Applied in conjunction with own team to: Engage the second opponent in defence Keep control of the game.
T	Reposition behind the barrier to stay in No.3 or become No.4: When in front of the ball If No.4 needs to be covered.

No.4	*Shuts the back door*
P	Be the last of the eight players on the field.
R	In attack make them give you the ball by: Staying behind the barrier to receive it Waiting for a secure chance to accelerate and hit the ball.
S	Maximise velocity to: Engage the first opponent in defence with or without the ball Interchange with own No.3 before he backhands.
T	Reposition as the last player on the field when: The ball, in attack, is behind you The attack of your team is about to fail.

THE BARRIER

There is a detailed description of the barrier on page 58 where it is explained that, with a continual awareness of its existence, all members of a polo team can be assisted to position correctly. In rugby union football a similar barrier separates the eight forwards in the scrum from the seven backs. The scrum half stands just behind the barrier as does the quarterback in American football and both have the same role as the No.3 in polo.

No.1 (see pages 20–25)

Often a beginner, or the least experienced player, has to be the No.1. Hence he badly needs to understand his job and have a clear system to help him fit in with the rest of the team. Application of LATET, especially watching and adjusting to his own No.3 behind the barrier, will greatly assist him to carry out the No.1's PRST.

There is confusion about the job of No.1. Some say it is to score goals, others insist that it is to mark the opposing No.4. I disagree with both views because, with balls bouncing, shots normally taken in a rush, and opponents looking for approach deviations to claim a foul, No.1 has more difficulties than the rest of the team when shooting at goal. On the other hand if No.1 spends all the game marking the opposing No.4, he will be completely left out of the attack, which must be wrong. Perhaps the best way to contain the opposing No.4 is to make him worry about No.1 in attack, and then, in defence, control him as defined under *Turn to Defence*.

In Tactics "A" (page 20), No.1 is given four jobs, one of which is to link to goal. Now linking becomes his main job, which is subdivided under PRST. Therefore if No.1 does score a goal it is a bonus to linking and, when in defence he marks the No.4 or last player, it is a part of maintaining the link because, at the same time, he should be adjusting for the reception of a backhand pass.

Many No.1s are abused by the other team members in the way that they send the ball upfield when there is no possibility of gaining possession, but then, if he has an opportunity to strike the ball, he is told "leave it". However, some No.1s are themselves to blame for not being involved because they are too far upfield or too central most of the time and also chase the ball at wrong moments. Sometimes the fault belongs to both the No.1 and the rest of the team, and the blame for a poor result should be shared. In any of the above three situations a coach could help enormously by correcting the wrongdoers and welding the team into a four man attack.

There is great pressure on a No.1 when in front of goal. The only way any player can learn to handle this is by experiencing this pressure frequently until he becomes accustomed to it and is given the opportunity to learn from making mistakes. It is even better if his contribution is criticised by, and discussed with, a coach. To be always uninvolved with attacks will provide no basis for discussion and achieve nothing. Instead he ought to be allowed to link to goal by positioning correctly, keeping the ball in play, giving his team velocity, and, in defence, marking the last opponent.

No.2 (see page 40)

The most difficult position in the team is No.2 because he must mark the best opponent and at the same time play a vital part in the attack. By achieving both, No.2 will be an effective link from the barrier to No.1, especially if he also fully applies LATET and PRST. But he will fail in his job if he selfishly tries for all the glory by shooting at goal without ever involving his No.1, or if he does not attempt to control his opposing No.3. Guidance from a sideline coach must help and would be essential if he is against an exceptionally good player.

A good method of increasing the control over the opposing No.3 is by using the tail trick against him whenever the game changes direction. How to do this is explained in Riding "C"

under the outward turn by a pair (page 64). This is useful as a ploy against anybody, but it will be even more valuable to control a strong No.3.

The key to all the above is accurate positioning. With poor concentration it is easy for a No.2 to slip into $1\frac{1}{2}$ or $2\frac{1}{2}$ instead of being the correct distance from his own No.3. From here passes can be received and redirected, the opposing No.3 controlled, and he will clearly see when his own No.3 requires covering.

No.3 (see page 59)

Unless he spends most of the time behind the barrier the No.3 cannot pivot effectively. From here he can control the defence, and launch, besides backing up, the attacks, applying LATET, PRST and the principles of the rope.

In too many polo teams the other three players do not know what their No.3 is doing. This is exacerbated by their failure to watch him sufficiently. Hence the opportunity to absorb some of the No.3's superior anticipation and to fully apply the team dimension of LATET is lost. As a result the No.3 can be forced to hit to himself and play individually because the other three are unable to adjust swiftly enough to be involved in either attack or defence. In some cases the No.3 is at fault by using his ability to hit the ball more than anyone else, thereby giving the rest of the team a minor role. This is basically wrong even if No.3 is by far the best player. Good teams share the ball between the four players employing tactics coordinated by No.3.

Quite often a combination of the two situations mentioned above exists in a team. Everyone is playing hard but there is little coordination between the pivot and the others. Only a sideline coach can rectify this with constructive directions. His aim would be that after discussion, practise and further playing experience, under his control, a better understanding between all the players should be achieved. For example at crucial moments the No.3 could slow down to allow the others to adjust to what they expect him to do. With ongoing practise and instruction a continual improvement can be expected.

To summarise: No.3 coordinates team tactics

by being the pivot from behind the barrier. From this position he distributes the ball using constructive angles, swiftly engages the second opponent in defence, and turns to defence whenever in front of the ball or barrier and if his No.4 needs covering.

No.4 (see pages 25–27)

This should be the easiest place to play, especially if the No.3 is helpful. It is simple for No.4 to stay last and watch the game unfold in front of him. With good self-discipline the back door can be kept shut and he will be able to participate in attacks by taking secure opportunities such as the reverse rope, but it is vital that PRST is applied in detail.

A bad No.4 is seldom last, joins the attack when he should not, often fouls opponents, and when out of position without the ball fails to return to be the last of his team. A good No.4 has the patience to wait as last player until given the ball, never fouls or gives any freedom to the opposing No.1, and after losing the ball in attack automatically returns to the No.4 position to defend.

A No.4 who is trusted to do his job as outlined in PRST will quickly grow in confidence. A shrewd coach will ensure that this happens and will then assess mistakes in a way that allows the No.4 to understand and learn from them.

Appendix I

THE RULES OF POLO

For permission to reproduce, in Appendices I, II and III, extracts from the rules of polo I am indebted to the Hurlingham Polo Association (H.P.A.). These rules are widely used and should be studied by all players of polo.

For reasons of space the full rules cannot be included here but I have quoted the basic ones and some recent amendments.

GENERAL RULES
Height of ponies
1 — Ponies of any height may be played.

Size of grounds
2 — *(a)* A full-sized ground shall not exceed 300 yards in length by 200 yards in width, if unboarded; and 300 yards in length by 160 yards in width, if boarded.

(b) The goals shall not be less than 250 yards apart, and each goal shall be 8 yards wide.

(c) The goal posts shall be at least 10 feet high, and light enough to break if collided with.

(d) The boards shall not exceed 11 inches in height.

Size of ball
3 — The size of the ball shall not exceed 3½ inches in diameter, and the weight of the ball shall be within the limits of 4¼ to 4¾ ounces.

Qualifications of players
4 — *(a)* The number of players is limited to 4 a side in all games and matches.

(b) No player may play under the influence of stimulative drugs.

(c) No player shall play with his left hand.

Note 1: No person shall play in any tournament or advertised match conducted by an Affiliated Club or Association in the British Isles unless:–

(i) He is an Associate Member of the H.P.A.

(ii) He has lodged a signed declaration, either with his Club or the H.P.A., to be bound by the rules, regulations, orders and directives of the H.P.A.

(iii) He is listed in the Association's current handicap list,

or has been allotted a handicap by the Association's Handicap Committee during the current season,

or his handicap has been confirmed by the Honorary Secretary of the Association.

Substitution
5 — *(a)* A player may only play in one team in the same tournament and in a tournament with the same "control number" in the fixture list, except as stated in *(e)* below.

(b) Substitutes must be qualified to play in the tournament and the team must remain qualified after the substitution has been made.

(c) A player who has taken part in one or more of the earlier rounds of a tournament, who is unable to play in a later round or rounds, may be replaced by a substitute. A member of a team who is unable to play in the earlier rounds of a tournament may also be replaced by a substitute.

(d) A player may be substituted for another during a match only if the latter player through sickness, accident or duty is unable to continue. If the substitute is of the same or lower handicap the score will not be altered, however if he is of a higher handicap the score will be immediately altered to reflect the increased aggregate handicap of the side irrespective of the period of play in which the substitution occurred.

(e) A Tournament Committee may agree to **any** player being used as a substitute provided:–

(i) They consider there is no suitable player (see Note 1) available who has not already played in the tournament or has been knocked out of a tournament with the same control number and is not due to play any further matches therein.

(ii) They are satisfied that there is a bona fide need for a substitute.

(iii) The total handicap of the team requiring a substitute will not be increased thereby, except in the circumstances described in *(d)* above. If a second substitute is brought into a team, it shall be the handicap the last time the team played which shall count.

(iv) In matches with an International flavour the captain of the opposing team's side agrees.

Notes on Substitution Rules

(1) A player shall be regarded as "suitable" if his handicap is not more than two goals less than the handicap of the player he is replacing.

(2) If a player is brought in in the case of an emergency for the completion of one match, he shall not be disqualified from continuing with his original team; he may continue to play with that team provided the original player is still not available and his own team is not still in the tournament.

(3) If a player is late and the game is started with a substitute, the late player may replace the substitute after the first chukka, but not thereafter.

(4) In the prospectus of a tournament with a subsidiary, it should be clearly stated whether or not both count as one tournament for the purposes of these rules.

Qualifications of ponies

6— (i) Ponies of any height may be played.

(ii) A pony blind in one eye may not be played (see Field Rule 3).

(iii) A pony may not be played which is not under proper control (see Field Rule 3).

(iv) In high and medium-goal tournaments, a pony played by one team cannot be played by any other team in the same tournament.

Notes:

(1) Attention is drawn to the H.P.A. Directive on the Misuse of Drugs and the Welfare of Ponies.

(2) In the British Isles all polo ponies must have a current certificate of vaccination.

Umpires, referees and goal judges

7— *(a)* The rules shall be administered in a match by two Umpires, who shall be mounted to enable them to keep close to the play, and a Referee who shall remain off the field of play in a central position. By mutual agreement between Captains of teams, one Umpire and if desired, also the Referee, may be dispensed with. The decision of the Umpire shall be final, except where there are two and they disagree, in which case the decision of the Referee shall be final.

(b) In important matches Goal Judges shall be appointed each of whom shall give testimony to the Umpires at the latter's request in respect to goals or other points of the game near his goal, but the Umpires shall make all decisions.

(c) The above Officials shall be nominated by the Committee conducting the tournament or match except in international matches when they shall be mutually agreed upon.

(d) Captains shall have the sole right to discuss with the Umpire or Umpires questions arising during the game. No player shall appeal in any manner to the Umpire or Umpires for fouls. This does not preclude a Captain from discussing any matter with the Umpire.

(e) The authority of the above Officials shall extend from the time the match is due to start until the end of the game. All questions arising at other times may be referred by the Captains to the Committee conducting the tournament or match and its decision shall be final.

Note: In the British Isles, except in international matches, every possible effort will be made to appoint at least one British Umpire. It is recommended that the referee is also British, and should be a regular past or present player in polo at least to the level being refereed.

Timekeeper and scorer

8—An official Timekeeper and Scorer shall be employed in all games and matches.

Doctors and veterinarians

9—At all organised polo games there will be a doctor and/or paramedic and a veterinary surgeon either present or on immediate call. A wagon equipped with screen must also be provided.

Duration of play

10—*(a)* The duration of play is 42 minutes divided into 6 periods of 7 minutes each. The number of minutes played in a period, or periods played in a match, may be reduced by the Committee conducting the tournament or match. In all matches there shall be a half-time interval of 5 minutes. All other intervals between periods shall be of three minutes' duration.

Handicap calculation

(b) In all matches played under handicap conditions the higher handicapped team shall concede to the lower handicapped team the difference in the handicaps divided by six and multiplied by the number of periods of play of the match. All fractions of a goal shall count as 'half-a-goal'. Mistakes in handicaps or in computing goal allowances must be challenged before a match begins, and no objection can be entertained afterwards.

Play continuous

(c) With the exception of the said intervals, play shall be continuous, and no time shall be taken off for changing ponies during a period, except as legislated for in Field Rule 23.

Termination of period

(d) Each period of play, except the last, shall terminate after the expiration of the prescribed time (designated by the ringing of the bell or other signal) as soon as the ball goes out of play or hits the boards.

A bell or other signal will be sounded 30 seconds after the first bell or signal, if the ball is still in play, and the period will terminate at the first sound of the second bell or other signal, although the ball is still in play, wherever the ball may be.

Penalty exacted next period

(e) If a foul is given after the first stroke of the 7 minute bell, the Umpire's whistle terminates the period, and the penalty shall be exacted at the beginning of the next period, except in the event of a tie in the last period when the penalty shall be exacted at once, and the period continued until the ball goes out of play or hits the boards or the 30 seconds bell is sounded.

Game stopped

(f) The game can be stopped in two different ways:-

(i) Where the time during which the game is stopped is *not* to be counted as part of the playing time of the period (*i.e.* where the clock is to be stopped). To indicate this to the Timekeeper the Umpire should blow one firm blast.·This way is used for fouls, Penalty 7 and under Field Rules 11, 14, 21 and 23. The ball is dead until the Umpire says "Play", and the ball is hit or hit at.

(ii) Where the time during which the game is stopped is to be counted as part of the playing time of the period (*i.e.* where the clock is *not* to be stopped). This occurs when the ball goes out of play, through the goal or over the boards, side or back lines (unless hit over the back line by a defender). As a rule the game will automatically stop, but if it continues (*e.g.* if the ball is hit straight into play after crossing the back or side lines), the Umpire should blow two sharp blasts. This will tell the Timekeeper not to deduct time.

Last period

(g) The last period shall terminate

although the ball is still in play, at the first stroke of the 7 minute bell, wherever the ball may be, except in the case of a tie.

(h) In the case of a tie the last period shall be prolonged till the ball goes out of play or hits the boards, or till the 30 seconds bell rings, and if still a tie, after an interval of five minutes the game shall be started from where the ball went out of play and be continued in periods of the usual duration, with the usual intervals, until one side obtains a goal, which shall determine the match.

Widened goals

(i) In the event of a tie at the end of the final period of a match goals will be widened for the ensuing periods:-

   (a) If the tournament conditions state that this will be so, or
   (b) If the captains of both teams concerned request that they should be.

In any event goals will be widened if no goal has been scored by the end of the first period of extra time.

Rules for widened goals:-

(i) Width of goals to be doubled to 16 yards by moving goal posts 4 yards outwards.
(ii) After a five minutes' interval ends shall be changed and the ball thrown in from the centre in the first of the extra chukkas.

Note: Committees are advised to put in the sockets to hold the goal posts at the 4-yard extensions before the tournament begins.

Prolongation in case of penalty

(j) In the event of a penalty being awarded within 20 seconds of the end of the match, the Timekeeper shall allow 20 seconds play from the time the ball is hit, or hit at, in carrying out the penalty, before he rings the final (7 minute) bell. If a goal is scored after the ball has been put into play, the final bell shall be rung, if the original regular time (7 minutes) has expired. The match shall terminate as usual on the first stroke of the final (7 minute) bell.

Unfinished match

(k) Once a match has started it shall be played to a finish unless stopped by the Umpire for some unavoidable cause, which prevents a finish the same day, such as darkness or the weather, in which case it shall be resumed at the point at which it has stopped, as to score, period and position of the ball, at the earliest convenient time, to be decided upon by the Committee conducting the tournament.

How game is won

11—The side that scores most goals wins the game.

Polo helmet or cap

12—No one shall be allowed to play unless he wears a protective polo helmet or polo cap, either of which must be worn with a chin strap.

Confusing colours

13—If in the opinion of the Tournament Committee the colours of two competing teams are so alike as to lead to confusion, the team lower in the draw or second named in a league competition shall be instructed to play in some other colours.

FIELD RULES

Definition of foul

1—Any infringement of the Field Rules constitutes a foul and the Umpire may stop the game.

Dead ball

2—The Umpire shall carry a whistle, which he shall blow when he wishes to stop the game. When he does so the ball is dead until he says "Play", and the time it is dead and not counted in the playing time of the period, except as legislated for in General Rule 10 (*f*).

Note: If a whistle is blown for a foul at approximately the same time as a goal is scored:-

   (i) The goal will be disallowed if the foul was against the attacking side and the foul was confirmed.
   (ii) The goal will be allowed if the foul was against the attacking side and the foul

is over-ruled; or if the foul was against the defending side whether or not the foul is confirmed.

Disqualified ponies

3 — A pony blind of an eye may not be played; a pony showing vice, or not under proper control, shall not be allowed in the game.

Note: In the British Isles all polo ponies must have a current certificate of flu vaccination.

Equipment for ponies

4 — (a) Protection of ponies by boots or bandages on all four legs is compulsory.

(b) Blinkers are not allowed, nor any form of noseband which obstructs the vision.

(c) Rimmed shoes are allowed, but the rim may only be on the inside of the shoe.

(d) Frost nails and screws are not allowed, but a calkin, fixed or movable is permissible, provided this is placed only at the heels of the hind shoes. The fixed or movable calkin shall be limited in size to a half inch cube.

(e) Hackamores or bitless bridles will not be used in matches or tournaments.

Note: The movable calkin is allowed so that when it becomes worn it can be replaced by a fresh one without re-shoeing. The essence of this permission is that the movable calkin should resemble, as far as possible, the recognised form of fixed calkin, and it does not permit the fixing of any fancy shaped spike, nor the placing of the calkin anywhere except at the heels of the hind shoes.

Disqualified equipment for players

5 — (a) Sharp spurs are not allowed.

(b) No player may wear buckles or studs on the upper part of his polo boots or knee pads in such a way as could damage another player's boots or breeches.

Safety zone

6 — (a) No person is allowed on the ground during play for any purpose whatever except the players and the Umpires. A player requiring a stick, pony or other assistance from an outside person must ride to the boards, side or back lines, to procure it. No person may come on to the ground to assist him.

(b) No person is allowed within the safety zone during play except those playing, umpires, referee, goal judges, manager and stickholders.

Note: The safety zone is an area including the field of play, the ground within about 10 yards of the boards and the ground within about 30 yards of the goal line.

Start of game

7 — At the beginning of the game the two teams shall line up in the middle of the ground, each team being on its own side of the half-way line. The Umpire shall bowl the ball underhand and hard between the opposing ranks of players, from a distance of not less than five yards, the players remaining stationary until the ball has left his hand.

How goal is scored

8 — A goal is scored when a ball passes between the goal posts and over and clear of the goal line. If a ball is hit above the top of the goal posts, but in the opinion of the Umpire between those posts produced, it shall count as a goal.

Changing of ends

9 — (a) Ends shall be changed every goal except where a goal is awarded under Penalty 1. Ends shall also be changed if no goals have been hit by half-time (in a seven or five period match, after the fourth or third period respectively), and play shall be re-started at a position corresponding to the change of ends. After a goal has been hit, the game shall be re-started from the middle of the ground as prescribed by Field Rule 7. The players shall be allowed a reasonable time in which to reach the middle of the ground at a slow trot and take up their positions.

Wrong line-up

(b) If the Umpire inadvertently permits lining up the wrong way the responsibility rests with him, and there is no redress; but if at the end of the period no goal has been scored the ends shall then be changed.

Attackers hit behind

10 — (a) The ball must go over and be clear of the back line to be out.

(b) When the ball is hit behind the back line by the attacking side, it shall be hit in by the defenders from the spot where it crossed the line, but at least four yards from the goal posts or boards, when the Umpire says "Play". None of the attacking side shall be within 30 yards of the back line until the ball is hit or hit at; the defenders being free to place themselves where they choose.

Unnecessary delay

(c) The defenders shall give the attacking side reasonable time to get into position, but there shall be no unnecessary delay in hitting in. In the event of unnecessary delay the Umpires shall call on the offending side to hit in at once. If the Umpire's request is not complied with, he shall bowl in the ball underhand and hard, at the spot where the ball crossed the back line and at right angles to it.

Defenders hit behind

11 — If the ball is hit behind the back line by one of the defending side, either directly or after glancing off his own pony, or after glancing off the side boards, Penalty 6 shall be exacted. If the ball strikes any other player or his pony before going behind, it shall be hit in in accordance with Field Rule 10.

Ball hit out

12 — (a) The ball must go over and clear the side lines or boards to be out.

(b) When the ball is hit over the boards or side line, it must be bowled, underhand and hard, by the Umpire into the ground from a point just inside the boards or lines where it went out, on an imaginary line parallel to the two goal lines, and between the opposing ranks of players, each side being on its own side of the imaginary line. No player may stand within 10 yards of the side lines or boards. Players must remain stationary until the ball has left the Umpire's hand. A reasonable time must be allowed players in which to line up.

Restarting after interval

13 — On play being resumed after an interval, the ball shall be put in play in the normal manner which would have been followed had there been no interval, *i.e.* in accordance with Field Rules 9, 10, 12 or 26, as the case may be. If the ball hits the side boards without going over them at the end of the previous period, it shall be treated as though it had been hit over them as laid down in Field Rule 12. The Umpire must not wait for players who are late.

Note: General Rule 10 (e) deals with resuming play when a period ends with a foul.

Damaged ball

14 — If the ball be damaged or trodden into the ground, the Umpire shall, at his discretion, stop the game and re-start it with a new ball, in the manner prescribed in Field Rule 26.

Note: It is desirable that the game shall be stopped and the ball changed when the damaged ball is in such a position that neither side is favoured thereby.

Carrying the ball

15 — A player may not catch, kick or hit the ball with anything but his stick. He may block with any part of his body but not with an open hand. He may not carry the ball intentionally. If the ball becomes lodged against a player, his pony or its equipment, in such a way that it cannot be dropped immediately, the Umpire shall blow his whistle and restart the game in accordance with Field Rule 26 at the point where it was first carried.

CROSSING

16 — The right of way

(a) (i) At each moment of the game there shall exist a Right of Way, which shall be considered to extend ahead of the player entitled to it, and in the direction in which he is riding.

No player shall enter or cross this Right of Way except at such a distance that not the slightest risk of a collision or danger to either player is involved.

(a) (ii) The Right of Way, which is defined in paragraphs (c) to (e) below, is not to be confused with the line of the ball and does not depend on who last hit it.

The line of the ball

(b) (i)   The line of the ball is the line of its course or that line produced at any moment.

(b) (ii)   If the line of the ball changes unexpectedly, for example when a ball glances off a pony, and as a result the Right of Way changes, the player who had the Right of Way must be given room to continue a short distance on his original Right of Way.

(b) (iii)   When a dead ball has been put into play through being hit at and missed the line of the ball is considered to be the direction in which the player was riding when he hit at it.

(b) (iv)   If the ball becomes stationary while remaining in play, the line of the ball is that line upon which it was travelling before stopping.

Player riding in direction ball is travelling

(c) (i)   A player following the ball on its exact line and taking it on his offside, is entitled to the Right of Way over all other players.

(c) (ii)   Where no player is riding on the exact line of the ball, the Right of Way belongs to the player following it on the smallest angle, provided he does not contravene Clause *(f)*.

(c) (iii)   Two players when following the exact line of the ball attempting to ride one another off, share the Right of Way over all other players.

(c) (iv)   A player riding in the direction the ball is travelling at an angle to its line, has the Right of Way over a player riding to meet the ball at an angle to its line, irrespective of the width of the angle provided he does not contravene Clause *(f)*.

(c) (v)   No player shall be deemed to have the Right of Way by reason of his being the last striker if he shall have deviated from pursuing the exact line of the ball.

Equal angles

(d)   In the rare case of two players riding in the general direction of the ball at exactly equal angles to it on opposite sides of its line, the Right of Way belongs to that player who has the line of the ball on his offside. The same rule applies as between players meeting the ball at exactly equal angles from the opposite sides of its line.

Player meeting the ball

(e) (i)   A player who rides to meet the ball on its exact line has the Right of Way over all players riding at an angle from any direction.

(e) (ii)   As between players riding to meet the ball, that player has the Right of Way whose course is at the least angle to the line of the ball.

Player to take ball on offside

(f)   The Right of Way entitles a player to take the ball on the offside of his pony. If he places himself to hit it on the near side and thereby in any way endangers another player who would otherwise have been clear, he loses the Right of Way and must give way to this other player.

(g)   When two players are riding from exactly opposite directions to hit the ball each shall take it on the offside of his pony. If a collision appears probable the player who has the Right of Way must be given way to.

Checking

(h) (i)   No player may check or pull up either on or across the Right of Way if by so doing he runs the slightest risk of collision with the player entitled to it.

(h) (ii)   If a player enters safely on the Right of Way and does not check, a player must not ride into him from behind, but must take the ball on the nearside of his own pony.

(h) (iii)   If a player with possession of the ball or right to the line of the ball on his offside, checks his speed to such an extent that an opposing player may enter the line and take the ball on his offside, without, in the opinion of the Umpires, creating any danger to the checking player, if that player were to *maintain* his reduced speed, then no foul shall be deemed to

have occurred, even if the checking player subsequently increases his speed. Umpires are advised that if the checking player slows to a walk or stops completely, under this directive, it is almost impossible for any danger to occur and therefore no foul is committed.

Dangerous riding

17 — A player may ride off an opponent, but he may not ride dangerously, as for example:

(*a*) Bumping at an angle dangerous to a player, or his pony.

(*b*) Zigzagging in front of another player riding at a gallop, in such a way as to cause the latter to check his pace or risk a fall.

(*c*) Pulling across or over a pony's legs in such a manner as to risk tripping the pony, etc.

(*d*) Riding an opponent across the Right of Way.

(*e*) Riding at an opponent in such a manner as to intimidate and cause him to pull out, or miss his stroke, although no foul or cross actually occurs.

(*f*) "Sandwiching", i.e. two players of the same team riding off an opponent at the same time.

Use of the Whip

18 — The whip may not be used unnecessarily or excessively.

Rough handling

19 — No player shall seize with the hand, strike, or push with the head, hand, forearm or elbow, but a player may push with his arm, above the elbow, provided the elbow be kept close to the side.

Misuse of stick

20 — (*a*) No player may hook an opponent's stick, unless he is on the same side of the opponent's pony as the ball, or in a direct line behind, and his stick is neither over or under the body or across the legs of an opponent's pony, nor may any player hook or strike at an opponent's stick unless all of the opponent's stick is below the opponent's shoulder level. The stick may not be hooked or struck unless the opponent is in the act of striking the ball.

(*b*) No player may reach immediately over and across or under and across any part of an opponent's pony to strike at the ball, nor may he hit into or amongst the legs of an opponent's pony, but if a player rides from behind into the backhander of the player who has the Right of Way, he does so at his own risk and there is no foul.

(*c*) No player may intentionally strike his pony with his polo stick.

(*d*) No player may use his stick dangerously, or hold it in such a way as to interfere with another player or his pony.

(*e*) No player may knowingly strike the ball after the whistle.

Note: If a hit occurs after the whistle for a foul, the Umpire may increase the severity of the penalty if the hit is by a member of the fouling team, or cancel the penalty or decrease its severity if the hit is by a member of the team fouled.

Loss of headgear

21 — If a player loses his headgear the Umpire shall stop the game to enable him to recover it, but not until an opportunity occurs that neither side is favoured thereby.

Dismounted player

22 — No dismounted player may hit the ball or interfere in the game.

Accident or injury

23 — (*a*) If a pony falls or goes lame, or if a player or pony be injured, or in the case of an accident to a pony's gear which in the opinion of the Umpire involves danger to the players or other players, the Umpire shall stop the game.

(*b*) If a player falls off his pony, the Umpire shall not stop the game, unless he is of the opinion that the player is injured. What constitutes a fall is left to the decision of the Umpire.

(*c*) When the game has been stopped in accordance with Clause (*a*) above, the Umpire shall re-start the game in the manner laid down in Field Rule 26, directly the player concerned is ready to resume play. The

Umpire shall not wait for any other player who may not be present.

(d) If a player be injured, a period not exceeding 15 minutes shall be allowed for his recovery. If the injured player is unfit to play after 15 minutes, the game shall be restarted with a substitute in place of the injured player, unless Penalty 8 has been exacted. If, however, the injured player subsequently recovers he may replace the player who was substituted in his place, but the handicap of the higher handicapped player will be counted in accordance with General Rule 5 *(d)*.

(e) In the event of a player being, or seeming to be, concussed, the following action will be taken. The Umpires, or if no Umpires are present, the senior player on the ground will stop the game and arrange for the player to see a doctor as soon as possible. The player will not be permitted to play again for a minimum of one week without a certificate of fitness from the official medical officer of his club. If no doctor is present when the accident occurred it will be the sole responsibility of the Umpires or the senior player present to decide if the player was actually concussed.

Disablement
24 — If a player be disabled by a foul so that he is unable to continue, Penalty 8 may be exacted, or the side which has been fouled shall have the option of providing a substitute. Penalty 1, 2 or 3 shall be exacted in any case.

When game is not stopped
25 — It shall be within the discretion of the Umpire not to stop the game for the purpose of inflicting a penalty, if the stopping of the game and the infliction of the penalty would be a disadvantage to the fouled side.

Re-starting when ball was not out
26 — If for any reason the game has to be stopped without the ball going out of play, it shall be re-started in the following manner. The Umpire shall stand at the spot where the ball was when the incident occurred, and facing the nearer side of the ground, but not nearer the boards or side lines than 20 yards.

Both teams shall take up their positions, each team being on its own side of an imaginary line, parallel to the goal lines and extending through the Umpire to the sides of the ground. No player may stand within five yards of the Umpire. The Umpire shall bowl the ball, underhand and hard, between the opposing ranks of players, towards the nearer side of the ground, the players remaining stationary until the ball has left his hand.

Discretion of umpires
27 — *(a)* Should any incident or question not provided for in the Rules of Polo, or the supplementary Rules of the Polo Association concerned, arise in a match, such incident or question shall be decided by the Umpire or Umpires. If the Umpires disagree, the Referee's decision shall be final.

(b) There are degrees of dangerous play and unfair play which give the advantage to the side fouling. The penalty to be inflicted is left to the discretion of the Umpire or Umpires and shall only be referred to the Referee in the event of the Umpires disagreeing on the penalty.

PENALTIES
Note: In all free hits the ball shall be considered in play the moment it has been either hit or hit at and missed.

Penalty goal
1 — *(a)* If, in the opinion of the Umpire, a player commits a dangerous or deliberate foul in the vicinity of goal in order to save a goal, the side fouled shall be allowed one goal.

(b) The game shall be re-started at a spot ten yards from the middle of the fouler's goal in the manner prescribed in Field Rule 26. Ends shall not be changed.

30-yard hit
2 — *(a)* A free hit at the ball from a spot 30 yards from the goal line of the other side fouling opposite the middle of the goal or, if preferred, from where the foul occurred (the choice to rest with the Captain of the side fouled); all the side fouling to be behind their

back line until the ball is hit or hit at, but not between the goal posts, nor when the ball is brought into play may any of the side ride out from between the goal posts; none of the side fouled to be nearer the goal line or back line than the ball is, at the moment it is hit, or hit at. In the event of the Captain of the side fouled electing to take the penalty from the spot where the foul occurred none of the defending side to be within 30 yards of the ball, nor come out from between the goal posts.

(b) In carrying out Penalty 2, if the free hit would, in the opinion of the Umpire, have resulted in a goal, but is stopped by one of the side fouling coming out from between the goal posts, or crossing the back line before the ball was struck, such shot is to count as a goal to the side fouled. If the player who stopped the ball did not infringe these rules, but another member of his side did, Penalty 7 (a) shall be exacted.

40-yard hit

3 — (a) A free hit at the ball from a spot 40 yards from the goal line of the side fouling opposite the middle of goal; all the side fouling to be behind their back line until the ball is hit or hit at, but not between the goal posts, nor when the ball is brought into play may any of the side ride out from between the goal posts; none of the side fouled to be nearer the goal line or back line than the ball is at the moment it is hit or hit at.

(b) In carrying out Penalty 3, if the free hit would, in the opinion of the Umpire, have resulted in a goal, but is stopped by one of the side fouling coming out from between the goal posts, or crossing the back line before the ball was struck, such shot is to count as a goal to the side fouled. If the player who stopped the ball did not infringe these rules, but another member of his side did, Penalty 7 (a) shall be exacted.

60-yard hit (opposite goal)

4 — A free hit at the ball from a spot 60 yards from the goal line of the side fouling opposite the middle of goal, none of the side fouling to

be within 30 yards of the ball, the side fouled being free to place themselves where they choose.

Free hit from the spot

5 — (a) A free hit at the ball from where it was when the foul took place, but not nearer the boards or side lines than four yards. None of the side fouling to be within 30 yards of the ball, the side fouled being free to place themselves where they choose.

Free hit from the centre

(b) A free hit at the ball from the centre of the ground, none of the side fouling to be within 30 yards of the ball, the side fouled being free to place themselves where they choose.

60-yard hit (opposite where ball crossed)

6 — A free hit at the ball from a spot 60 yards distant from the back line, opposite where the ball crossed it, but not nearer the boards or side lines than four yards. None of the side fouling to be within 30 yards of the ball; the side fouled being free to place themselves where they choose.

Another hit

7 — (a) If the side fouling fail to carry out Penalty 2, 3, 4, 5 or 6 correctly the side fouled shall be allowed another free hit at the ball, unless a goal has been scored or awarded. If both sides fail to carry out Penalty 2 or 3 correctly, another free hit must be taken by the side fouled, irrespective of the result of the previous free hit.

Hit in by defenders

(b) If the side fouled fail to carry out Penalty 2 or 3 correctly, the defenders shall be allowed a hit in from the middle of their own goal. None of the attacking side shall be within 30 yards of the back line until the ball is hit, or hit at; the defenders being free to place themselves where they choose.

Hit in from 30-yard line

(c) If the attacking side fail to carry out Field Rule 10 correctly the defenders shall be allowed to hit in from the 30-yard line, from the spot opposite where the first hit was made or would have been made. None of the attackers shall be within 30 yards of the ball until it is hit or hit at; the defenders being free to place themselves where they choose. For infringement of Penalty 7 *(b)* or any further infringement of Penalty 7 *(c)* by the attacking side, the defenders shall be allowed another hit in from the 30-yard line.

Unnecessary delay

(d) In the event of unnecessary delay by the side fouled when called on by the Umpire to take a penalty hit, the Umpire shall restart the game from the spot where the hit should have been taken in accordance with Field Rule 26.

Player to retire

8 — Designation by the Captain of the side fouled of the player on the side fouling whose handicap is nearest above that of the disabled player, who shall retire from the game. If the handicap of the disabled player is higher than that of any of his opponents the player whose handicap is nearest below that of the disabled player may be designated. If there are two or more such players the Captain of the side fouled shall designate the one to retire. The game shall be continued with three players on each side, and if the side fouling refuses to continue the game, it shall thereby forfeit the match. This penalty does not apply to international matches.

Pony disqualified

9 — *(a)* For infringement of Field Rule 3; the pony ordered off the ground by the Umpire and disqualified from being played again during the game or match.

Note: The case of a pony blind of an eye must be reported by the Umpire in writing to the Committee conducting the tournament who shall take all steps necessary to ensure that it shall not be played again in any tournament.

Pony ordered off

(b) For infringement of Field Rule 4; the pony ordered off the ground by the Umpire and disqualified from playing again until the offence has been removed.

Player ordered off

(c) For infringement of Field Rule 5; the player ordered off the ground by the Umpire and disqualified from playing again until he has removed the offence.

General Note: In all the above three cases play must be re-started immediately as prescribed in Field Rule 26 and the game shall continue while the player is changing his pony or removing the offence.

Player excluded

10 — The Umpire may exclude a player from the game, in addition to any other penalty, in the case of a deliberate, dangerous foul, or conduct prejudicial to the game. Alternatively, for a less serious offence, he may exclude a player for the rest of the chukka in progress. The side to which the excluded player belonged shall continue with three players only, or forfeit the match.

Note: The circumstances which caused this penalty to be inflicted must be reported by the Umpire in writing to the Committee conducting the tournament, to enable them to judge whether the case should be reported to higher authority.

NOTES FOR UMPIRES AND OTHER OFFICIALS

THE REFEREE

General Rule 7 *(a)*, states: The Rules shall be administered in a match, by two Umpires, who shall be mounted to enable them to keep close to the play, and a Referee who shall remain off the field of play in a central position. By mutual agreement between Captains of teams, one Umpire and, if desired, also the Referee, may be dispensed with. The decision of the Umpire shall be final, except where there are two, and they disagree, in which case the decision of the Referee shall be final.

The task of the Referee is a very responsible one, and requires continual concentration throughout the game. In many matches he may never be asked for a decision; and then, suddenly, an occasion arises when the Umpires disagree and come to the Referee for a ruling, and a definite and final opinion must be given. The Referee should, therefore, have had considerable experience of good polo, and, if possible, of umpiring. He should not only know the Rules well, but be able to refer to any Rule quickly. He should always have the Book of Rules beside him.

When the Umpires appeal to him to decide whether a foul occurred or not, the Referee should confine his decision to this point, as laid down in Field Rule 27 *(b)*. The Referee should refrain from allocating a penalty unless specifically asked to do so.

The Referee should sit in a central position, at the side of the ground, *apart from distracting influences*, from which position he can see clearly and be easily accessible to the Umpires, who should know his exact position before play begins.

The Rules allow for a Referee when there is only one Umpire. In this case the Referee's duties are quite different; instead of arbitrating in case of disagreement between the Umpires he now has to act as a second Umpire to whom the mounted Umpire can appeal for assistance to decide cases in which he may not be able to see sufficiently clearly the degree of danger in a foul, etc.

Whenever possible the referee should be a regular past or present player in polo at least to the level of the game he is refereeing. In the British Isles he should, where possible, be from the U.K.

Hand signals
The following hand signals are used in order to reduce the time taken in discussions between the Umpires and the Referee.

(a) The Umpires having consulted each other, turn towards the Referee and one of them raises his hand (this is to show that they disagree).

(b) If, in the Referee's opinion, no foul occurred, he will make the wash-out signal by a horizontal movement of both arms across his front.

(c) If he thinks a foul has occurred and it is obvious which side fouled, he will raise one hand above his head and point in the direction the hit is to be taken with the other.

(d) If he is in any doubt whatsoever about any aspect of the affair, he will stand up but will make no signal at all, upon which the Umpires will canter up to consult him.

(e) The Umpires may wish to consult him in any case, in which case they will naturally canter straight up to him without making any signals.

(f) There is no reason why the Umpires should not ask the Referee which side fouled if they are in any doubt.

THE UMPIRES
1 Ponies
Official and voluntary Umpires in every class of polo must be adequately mounted. They should be sufficiently well mounted to enable them to keep close to the game without having to think of riding their ponies. The practice of umpiring on young ponies in order to school them is strongly deprecated.

2 Umpires' duties before game begins

(a) It is important that at advertised games at Polo Clubs, where public money is being taken, the game should start at the time advertised. Whilst this is really the business of the Polo Manager in a big Club, Umpires should be ready strictly on time and should ride out to the centre of the ground two minutes before the game is due to start.

(b) The Umpires should check the following points before throwing the ball in:

(i)   Who the Referee is and where he is sitting.

(ii)   That the timekeeper and Goal Judges are in position.

(iii)   In handicap matches that the handicap is correctly put up and that both sides are satisfied with it, General Rule 10 *(b)*.

(iv)   That they both, as well as the timekeeper, fully understand General Rule 7 *(f)*.

(v)   That one of the Umpires should be prepared to toss for choice of goals on the arrival of the teams.

3 Positions

(a) Division of ground

Before going on the ground Umpires should mutually agree to take a side line and a back line each. It is suggested that they should change sides at half time or by matches, as, if a polo ground is correctly laid out, it means that one Umpire is facing the sun the whole afternoon.

While it is obvious that one Umpire must be responsible for throwing in from one side line to the other, it must be clearly understood that the responsibility for blowing the whistle for an infringement of the Rules in any portion of the ground is co-equal.

An Umpire on one side of the ground must not hesitate to blow his whistle if he sees a Rule being broken towards the other side of the ground; even in the near vicinity of the other Umpire, for that other Umpire may at the moment be unsighted by having ponies between him and the foul, or he may unavoidably miss it through being in the act of turning.

(b) Hit-in

It is essential also that the one Umpire should be behind the back line when the ball is hit from behind. If an Umpire is standing behind a player hitting in from behind he will see the exact line of the ball in whatever direction it is being hit and will get a very clear view of any opposing player coming to meet the hit-in.

This meeting of the hit-in forms one of the most frequent causes of crossing, and it is important that the exact line of the ball should be observed; the other Umpire should be keeping his eye on the 30-yard line to see that the opponents of the side hitting in do not cross the line before the ball is hit or hit at.

(c) Penalties 2 and 3

It is even more essential that one Umpire should be on the goal line in 30 and 40 yard hits as the defending side may not cross the back line until the ball is hit or hit at, or come out between the goal posts. Infringement of this Rule has such strong penalties that it is obvious that an Umpire should be on the goal line, otherwise it will be impossible to detect this infringement.

(d) Penalties 4 and 5 (a) and (b)

In the case of the 60-yard hits and the free hits (in the event of the latter being fairly near goal) it is also important that an Umpire should be close behind the line in the melees which frequently result from those penalties close in front of goal, the hooking of sticks on the wrong side often occurs, and the defenders may hit behind and it is difficult to see unless the Umpire is close.

(e) It follows that if these positions are mutually agreed to by the two Umpires, the general position of the two Umpires, whatever direction the game goes in, will be that one Umpire will be more or less at a short distance behind the game while the other is galloping level with it. It is considered that this is the ideal combination of the two positions to make certain of seeing every possible infringement of the Rules.

4 Use of Whistle—General Rule 10 (f)

(a) Be careful to use the whistle correctly. Re-

member there is a timekeeper who has to stop the clock when you blow one firm blast, but who must not stop the clock when you blow two sharp blasts. Read General Rule 10 *(f)* carefully and note the occasions when to blow one firm blast and when to blow two sharp ones. In both cases the ball is dead until you say "Play" (Field Rule 2), but in the latter case the time it is dead counts in the playing time of the period and in the former it does not: you must be very careful to blow the whistle in the correct manner. Although you should not normally blow the whistle when the attacking side hit behind you must be on the lookout to do so if the defending side hit behind, as this will entitle the attackers to a 60-yard hit opposite where the ball crossed.

(b) The Umpire should carry his whistle in his hand ready for instant use and must make-up his mind in a flash and blow without hesitation. Owing to the pace at which polo is played, any momentary delay is fatal, as situations change so rapidly that an Umpire may end by not blowing his whistle at all for a foul that he really meant to give. A small stick with a whistle fitted at one end is recommended.

(c) The Umpire having blown his whistle should quickly check with the other Umpire that he agrees there was a foul and to the proposed penalty. This can be done either verbally or preferably by a nod of the head or some other prearranged signal—it is most important that there should be no delay through long discussion.

The Umpire should then loudly and clearly announce the foul and penalty, thus: "Cross against Red, free hit from the spot", and without waiting canter to the spot where the foul occurred, drop the ball and go to his position. There is no necessity to state the number of the penalty awarded.

5   *Concentration*

Owing to the speed at which it is played, polo is the most difficult of all games to Umpire. The Umpire must be concentrated on the play every moment of the period; he should be watching the game so closely that he is certain of the line of the ball each time it has been hit, and, conse-

quently, knows at a glance which player has the Right of Way. He must further establish the direction of the Right of Way (in his mind) bearing in mind that it is very likely that the Right of Way and the line of the ball will not coincide. The moment the line of the ball is changed he must quickly know who is now entitled to the Right of Way and in what direction the new Right of Way lies. Attention is drawn to Field Rule 16 *(b)* (ii). It is the Umpire's job to see that the player who has Right of Way is given sufficient room to pull up or turn when the Right of Way changes suddenly.

A common error among inexperienced Umpires is lack of concentration due to watching some brilliant individual or combined play, more from an appreciation of the players' point of view than as an Umpire.

6   *No appealing—general rule 7 (d)*

Captains shall have the sole right to discuss with the Umpire or Umpires any matter arising during the game: but no player shall appeal in any manner to the Umpire for fouls. This includes a player holding up his stick, for which he may be penalised after a warning under Field Rule 27. If thought necessary a general caution to all players should be given at the beginning of a match or chukka, after which any appeal for a foul may be penalised without further warning.

It is very necessary that there should be no hanging about or long discussions between Umpires, and the right of a Captain or a side to discuss matters with the Umpire does not include the right to challenge the Umpire's normal decisions.

Never get into an argument with the players. It is unnecessary to discuss anything with the players while playing; or explain reasons for giving any decisions; but, in the interests of the game, when it is finished a discussion of the game and the fouls that occurred will be found helpful, especially to young players.

7   *Prolongation in the event of a tie—*
   General Rule 10 (h)

Remember that if the game ends in a tie at the end of the final period the game must carry on after the bell is rung until the ball goes out of play or the 30-second bell is rung.

8   Allowing a goal after whistle
Read carefully Note to Field Rule 2 as to when a goal may be allowed to stand after the whistle is blown for a foul.

9   Field Rules 3, 4 and 5
The method of dealing with offences under these Rules is given in detail in Penalties 9 (a), (b) and (c) respectively. These offences concern unmanageable ponies, blinkers, frost nails, sharp spurs and protruding buckles on boots and knee pads. The Umpire should ride up to the Captain of the team and direct him to tell the player to change his pony or remove the offence.

Note that if a pony is disqualified (Penalty 9) (a) or a player is excluded (Penalty 10) a written report is required from the Umpire.

10   Changing ends—Field Rule 9
Remember that, if by half-time no goals have been scored, ends will be changed.

Remember also, that if a goal has been scored, it is laid down that teams should return to the centre at the pace of a slow trot. It will be found that in an exciting match, when the score is level or nearly level and the last period is being played, one team or the other, or both, will gallop back to the centre to get the ball thrown in. Remember to stick to the trot when returning to the throw-in.

11   Crossing—Field Rule 16
(a) It is difficult to lay down an exact distance as to what constitutes a cross, but in all doubtful cases the pace at which the players are moving must be considered, or whether there was any danger involved, as on this depends the question whether the player entitled to the Right of Way has to check to avoid a collision. The benefit of the doubt should be in favour of the man entitled to the Right of Way.

The good Umpire gets consistent in giving penalties for crossing, and this is more appreciated by the players than anything else.

(b) A frequent form of foul is committed by a player swinging his pony across the Right of Way immediately before or after hitting at the ball. This often occurs after taking a nearside backhander. Another foul under this Rule is checking for a backhander (even when the striker is entitled to the Right of Way) when an opponent is following close behind in full pursuit. On the other hand, once a player has safely taken over the Right of Way from another player, the latter may not ride into the former from behind unless the former checks his pony.

(c) Umpires are apt to forget that a player riding in the direction that the ball is travelling at an angle to its line, has the Right of Way over a player riding to meet the ball at an angle to its line, irrespective of the width of the angle, provided he takes the ball on his offside.

It is only when a player rides to meet the ball on its *exact* line that he has the Right of Way over all other players riding at an angle from any direction.

12   Dangerous angle—Field Rule 17 (a)
The Umpire when deciding whether a bump was made at a dangerous angle, should consider the speed at which the player was riding and whether the bump could have caused the pony to fall, for example a bump behind the saddle at an acute angle.

Players should straighten out almost parallel with their opponents before riding them off.

13   Intimidation—Field Rule 17 (e)
This Rule should be carefully read and strictly enforced.

14   Misuse of stick—Field Rule 20
The Rule states that the stick may be only hooked or struck when an adversary is *in the act* of striking at the ball and that a player is not allowed to strike or hook an opponent's stick above the level of the shoulder.

It should be noted that no player may strike at the ball among the legs of an adversary's pony and that the hind legs are included in this Rule. However, if a player rides into the backhander of a player entitled to the Right of Way, he does so at his own risk.

The same Rule states that no player shall

intentionally strike his pony with his polo stick. Under the HPA Rule a player is prohibited from intentionally striking his pony with the shaft or even thumping it with the butt end of the handle.

Some examples of dangerous use of stick are:

(a) Taking a full swing at the ball from the throw-in or in a scrimmage in such a way as to endanger other players.

(b) Striking hard into a group of ponies' legs during a scrimmage.

(c) Striking at the ball in the air so as to endanger other players.

(d) Taking a full swing under a pony's neck in such a way as to endanger a player riding alongside.

(e) Striking an opponent's stick in such a way as may cause injury to an opponent.

As a general rule Umpires are not sufficiently strict about giving these fouls.

15 *Accident or injury—Field Rule 23 (a)*

This Rule states: "If a pony falls or goes lame, or if a player or pony be injured, or in case of an accident to a pony's gear which, in the opinion of the Umpire, involves danger to a player, or other players, the Umpire shall stop the game."

For example the following can be considered:
Broken Martingale, if end trails on the ground.
Broken girth.
Broken reins, if single.
Broken headstall, allowing bit to fall out.
Loose bandages, or boots.

The game is not stopped for:
Broken Martingale, if *not* dangerous.
Lost or broken leathers.
Broken curb chain.
Lost bandages or boots.
Responsibility for deciding what is or not dangerous, however, must remain with the Umpire.

16 *When game is not stopped—Field Rule 25*

"It shall be within the discretion of the Umpire not to stop the game for the purpose of inflicting a penalty, if the stopping of the game and the infliction of the penalty would be to the disadvantage of the side fouled."

This is one of the most difficult rules to apply, for if the Umpire refrains from blowing his whistle because he thinks the striker is bound to get a goal, it is perfectly all right if he gets the goal, but should he miss, it is both unfortunate and awkward.

N.B.: Note to Field Rule 2.

17 *Discretion of umpires—Field Rule 27*

This Rule empowers Umpires to penalise all dangerous and unfair play and bad behaviour on the ground that it is not mentioned in the Rules.

18 *Penalties*

(a) There are no less than five separate penalty hits (Penalties 2 to 5 *(b)*):
The 30-yard Hit.
The 40-yard Hit.
The 60-yard Hit.
The Free Hit from the Spot.
The Free Hit from the Centre of the Ground.

As regards the actual penalties themselves: there are eleven. Umpires must know these by heart but there is no longer any need to know the numbers, since the Rules give the name of each penalty, which should be used in preference to the number.

Umpires must bear in mind that penalties should be both appropriate to the infringements which they penalise and consistent, in that the same penalty should always be awarded for infringements of similar type and gravity. Inconsistency is a major cause of friction between players and Umpires.

(b) Penalty 1

The ruling of a penalty goal states: "If, in the opinion of the Umpire, a player commits a dangerous or deliberate foul in the vicinity of goal in order to save a goal, the side fouled shall be allowed one goal."

The Umpire, having awarded a penalty goal, shall immediately instruct the goal judge to wave the white flag.

When throwing in from the spot ten yards in front of the goal it is preferable that the ball should be thrown in towards the side of the ground where the foul took place.

A clear definition is sometimes asked for as to what "vicinity" means in terms of distance from the goal.

The fact that the foul is considered to have been committed in order to save a goal obviously denotes that the player fouled is in a position to score, and is therefore, in most cases, close to the goal. It is difficult to lay down any actual distance to cover "vicinity", but this penalty goal has seldom been given at distances exceeding the 40-yard line unless the player fouled is more or less in front of goal and had an open run at the goal if he had not been fouled.

(c) Penalty 2

Remember that the wording for a 30-yard hit is: "A free hit at the ball from a spot 30 yards from the goal line of the side fouling, opposite the middle of the goal, or, if preferred, from where the foul occurred (the choice to rest with the Captain of the side fouled...)" ... It is, therefore, clear that an Umpire, if the foul occurs anywhere nearer the goal than 30 yards, should immediately ride up to the Captain of the side fouled and offer him the choice of a free hit from 30 yards or from the place where the foul occurred; he should not decide this matter himself, and he should remember that in the latter case the fouling side may not be within 30 yards of the ball, nor may they come out between the goal posts.

(d) Penalty 2 and 3

It is of utmost importance to remember that in carrying out 30 or 40 yard hits, if the hit would, in the opinion of the Umpires, have resulted in a goal, but is stopped by one of the side fouling coming out between the goal posts, or crossing the back line before the ball was struck, such a shot is to count as a goal to the side fouled. If the player who stopped the ball did not infringe these Rules, but another member of the side did, then the fouled side should be allowed another hit from the same position (Penalty 7 (a)).

This bears out the importance of one Umpire being on the goal line.

(e) Penalty 4 and 5 (a)

Remember that, in 60-yard hits and free hits from the spot and centre, the Umpires should see that the side fouling should stand back 30 yards from the ball before it is hit or hit at. In view of the fact that there are a large number of 60-yard hits, Umpires can train their eyes very quickly as to what 30 yards is, as there is a 30-yard line marked on the ground as well as a 60-yard line.

Remember that a free hit (i.e. from where the foul took place) can be as severe as a 30- to 40-yard hit, for it is clear that if an infringement of the Rules takes place, say, 15 yards in front of the goal for which the Umpire decides that a free hit is suitable, the side fouling must be 30 yards from the ball when it is hit or hit at, and will, therefore, be 15 yards behind the goal, thus making the goal almost a certainty; and if an infringement occurs calling for the exercise of a 60-yard hit opposite goal or a free hit from where the foul took place, at a point nearer the goal line than 60 yards, then a free hit from the spot should generally be given and the side fouled get the benefit of having the better chance of hitting a goal than if they had been given Penalty 4 and taken back to 60 yards. However, the gravity of the infringement must be the deciding factor in the Umpire's decision.

(f) Penalty 5 (b)

Umpires should bear in mind that the object in having both Penalty 5 (a), a free hit from the spot, and Penalty 5 (b), a free hit from the centre of the ground, is to give Umpires alternative penalties which may be awarded at their discretion.

In awarding these and other penalties the gravity of the infringement, where it took place and the direction of play must decide the severity of the penalty. Thus a Penalty 5 (b) may be awarded where a free hit from the spot is considered inadequate and a 60-yard hit would be too severe.

For example, where the attacking side commits an infringement near the defenders' back line the Umpires should award either a free hit from the spot or a free hit from the centre depending upon the gravity of the infringement.

They also have the more severe options of Penalties 4, 3 or 2 but would only award one of these in the case of a serious foul. Alternatively, where a defending team commits a minor or accidental infringement just within its own half then a free hit from the spot may be more appropriate than a Penalty 4.

Additionally, without overriding their general discretion, Umpires should take into account the direction of play when an infringement occurs. As a general rule if the attacking team is fouled it should at least be taken forward to the next most severe penalty, whilst if a defending player is fouled a free hit from the spot will often be appropriate.

19 Unnecessary delay

(a) Your attention is drawn to Penalty 7 (d) "Unnecessary Delay". The H.P.A. has decided that it will include "teeing-up" and circling.

(b) "Teeing-up" whether by the striker or another player, or both, will be taken to mean either making a "tee" or rolling the ball on to an existing "tee" (e.g., hoofprint).

(c) The ball may be moved by a player, but once it is lying on a flat surface of reasonable area it is ready to hit.

(d) The Umpire will allow reasonable time for this (say 2 or 3 seconds) and he will say "Play" as soon as he can, and will do so in any case if the player tries to "tee-up". If the striker does not then *immediately* begin to take the hit, the Umpire will blow his whistle and act as in Penalty 7 (d).

(e) As soon as the ball is touched or hit in any way after the order "Play", this will be taken to be the free hit.

(f) You are reminded that delay is sometimes caused deliberately, not only for the sake of "teeing-up", but also to allow a pony to be changed, etc. For this reason, the practice of circling to get on the right leading leg, or any reason, is also to be disallowed, either at the beginning or the run-up or at the end of it.

(g) Umpires attention is drawn to the rule that the interval between chukkas is 3 minutes. It is accepted that the 5 minute interval at half-time is not always enforceable due to the practice of "treading in".

20 Nearside offences
Taking the ball on the Nearside

The relevant rules on the subject are Field Rule 16(f) (player to take the ball on offside) which reads as follows:—

"The Right of Way entitles a player to take the ball on the offside of his pony. If he places himself to hit it on the nearside and thereby in any way endangers another player who would otherwise have been clear, he loses the Right of Way and must give way to this other player."

and Field Rule 17 (Dangerous Riding):—

(b) "Zigzagging in front of another player riding at a gallop in such a way as to cause the latter to check his pace or risk a fall."

(c) "Pulling across or over a pony's legs in such a manner as to risk tripping the pony, etc."

There is nothing in the Rules to prevent a player taking the ball on the nearside provided, as in any other manoeuvre, he does not endanger another player by doing so. It must be remembered that in high goal polo, the pace is faster than in low and medium, and the faster the horse is going, the longer it takes him to pull up. The safety distance in high goal polo is therefore greater than in low.

This manoeuvre can, of course, be penalised under Rule 16(f) or 17(b) and (c). Umpires are therefore directed that a player may move over and take the ball on the nearside, provided there is sufficient distance between him and the other player not to endanger the latter; the important words being in 16(f) "... and thereby endangers another player". The other guiding principle is that the faster the polo, the greater the safety distance that must be allowed.

It is, of course, a foul to take the ball on the nearside if an opponent is meeting it correctly, Rule 16(g).

21 Damaged ball

(a) Example. The ball splits into two parts and one part goes through the goal. If it is clear that the larger part of the ball goes through the goal the Umpires will normally award a goal. If the parts are about equal, the Umpires have to use their discretion and decide one way or the other.

If a goal is not awarded, Field Rule 14 may be applied.

(b) Example. The ball splits or breaks up when struck in the course of a penalty being taken. Umpires, in this case, should allow the penalty to be taken again. But presumably they may decide the ball has not broken up sufficiently and that the larger part is still in play or has gone through or past the goal.

22   Throw-ins
    (a) "Throw-ins" from the *centre.*
        (i)   Keep the players behind the mark.
        (ii) Stop them charging the Umpire.
        (iii) Keep 10 yards back from the mark.
    (b) "Throw-ins" from the *side.*
        (i)   Place your horse's *hind* legs on the side line.
        (ii) Keep the players a further 5 yards away from you.
        (iii) Keep them still.

(c) The ball should be thrown in underarm and hard.

THE TIMEKEEPER

General Rule 8 states: "An Official Timekeeper and Scorer shall be employed in all games and matches."

The length of each period is 7 minutes. The time during which a penalty is being exacted or an accident being dealt with does not count in the 7 minutes playing time. The fact that the time is not to be counted (i.e. the clock is to be stopped) is indicated by the Umpire blowing one firm blast on his whistle. The time starts to count again (i.e. the clock is to be started) when the Umpire says "Play" and the ball is hit or hit at.

The Timekeeper will find no difficulty in excluding the time required for penalties and accidents from the playing time of the period if he is provided with a proper polo stop-clock.

If none is available, two ordinary stop-watches will do, one being used to record the time from the commencement of the period and the other for noting the time to be added to the first watch on account of penalties and accidents.

The Timekeeper must note that if the Umpire blows two sharp blasts the time that the ball is dead is to be included in the playing time and, therefore, no action is required by the Timekeeper.

It is the Timekeeper's duty to ring the bell when the 7 minute period finishes, and again 30 seconds later if play has not already stopped. Great care must be taken that the first stroke of the ball coincides exactly with the termination of the 7 and 7½ minutes, for, in the case of a close match, in a final period, a ball may pass between the goal posts a second before or after the correct time of the conclusion of the period. The Timekeeper's responsibility in this matter is, therefore, of great importance.

Between each period there is an interval of 3 minutes. In all matches there is a half-time interval of 5 minutes. Should play begin before the 3 minutes are up, it is unnecessary to ring the bell but the clock should be started at the moment that play begins. If the play has not begun at the end of each interval the Timekeeper shall ring the bell, but he must not start the clock until play actually begins.

In the event of a tie requiring that an extra period be played, the interval shall be 5 minutes. In this case it is the Umpire's duty to see that the game is not started again until the 5 minutes interval has been taken.

General Rule 10 *(j)* is extremely important to the Timekeeper, as he is the only official who can carry out this rule. It reads: "In the event of a penalty being awarded within 20 seconds of the end of the match, the Timekeeper shall allow 20 seconds play from the time the ball is hit, or hit at, in carrying out the penalty, before he rings the final (7 minute) bell. If a goal is scored after the ball has been put into play, the final bell shall be rung, if the original regular time (7 minutes) has expired. The match shall terminate as usual on the first stroke of the final (7 minute) bell.

Thus, if the whistle blows for any foul committed when there is less than 20 seconds to go before time in the final period, it is the clear duty of the Timekeeper to allow 20 seconds more play from the time the ball is hit, or hit at, in taking the penalty. He needs a stop-watch capable of timing this 20 seconds.

The Timekeeper should be provided with a white flag. When the Goal Judge signals a goal by waving his white flag, the Timekeeper should acknowledge by waving his flag in reply; he must keep the score on a proper form, and see that the score is correctly put up on the board.

The Timekeeper should fully understand Penalty 1 (Penalty Goal), when the Umpire orders the Goal Judge to signal a goal as a result of a foul in the vicinity of goal, and throws in the ball to restart the game at a spot ten yards from the middle of the fouler's goal: also General Rule 10 *(f)*, (i) and (ii)—correct use of whistle.

In International and important Open Cup matches, Committees are recommended to appoint a member of the Committee, or designate some suitable official, to sit with the Timekeeper to assist him in his responsible duties.

THE GOAL JUDGES

The duty of signalling goals each end is usually undertaken by a member of the ground staff, and this duty is generally efficiently carried out.

General Rule 7 *(b)* reads: "In important matches Goal Judges shall be appointed each of whom shall give testimony to the Umpires at the latter's request in respect of goals or other points of the game near his goal, but the Umpires shall make all decisions."

A flag should be waved, when a goal is scored, until acknowledged by the Timekeeper.

This flag should be *kept down and furled* until a goal is scored.

Remember, an Umpire may order a Goal Judge to signal a goal for Penalty 1 without the ball having actually passed through the goal.

When the ball is hit behind, a Goal Judge should quickly place a new ball on the spot where it crossed the line, remembering that it must not be nearer than four yards to the goal posts or the side boards.

Remember, the Umpires may at any moment ask the Goal Judge's opinion on the question of whether the defending side hit the ball behind the goalline or on other points of the game near the goal. They, however, make all decisions.

Sometimes the ball rolls only a few inches over the goalline between the posts, or is hit back again by a defender just as it has crossed the line. This must be carefully watched for.

Goal Judges should wear white coats (long ones are not recommended), and keep out of the way of the players.

It is recommended that in important matches two Goal Judges should be appointed each end. They should be polo players, and energetic.

Many polo players and Umpires will remember difficult situations when a goal has been shot at from an acute angle, particularly if the ball has passed above the level of the goal posts. The normal single Goal Judge standing well back behind the centre of the goal, may be in doubt whether it was a goal, but must either signal a goal or not. The Umpire, whose decision is final, can intervene but may or may not have been in a position to see more clearly than the Goal Judge.

If two Goal Judges are posted each end such a situation should not occur. They can stand together behind the goal when the game is running towards the other goal; but the moment an attack on their goal is coming, one of them should always keep moving, so as to keep the approaching ball in view, through the goal posts, particularly when it is actually struck at goal.

UMPIRING DIRECTIVES

We re-publish below for convenience recent directives on Umpiring which represent the current practice:-

UNNECESSARY DELAY

Before season 1974, it was generally thought that there was too much "unnecessary delay" and in particular whilst a penalty was being taken. The HPA issued the following directive:-

"Teeing-up"

(a) The HPA has decided that this must be stopped. It causes most irritating delays.

(b) *No change in the Rules is necessary.* Your attention is drawn to Penalty 7 (d) "Unnecessary Delay". The Umpire's interpretation of "Unnecessary Delay" has become uncertain and the HPA has decided that it will include "teeing-up" and circling.

(c) "Teeing-up" whether by the striker or another player, or both, will be taken to mean either making a "tee" or rolling the ball on to an existing "tee" (e.g., hoofprint).

(d) The ball may be moved by a player, but once it is lying on a flat surface of reasonable area it is ready to hit.

(e) The Umpire will allow reasonable time for this (say 2 or 3 seconds) and he will say "Play" as soon as he can, and will do so in any case if the player tries to "tee-up". If the striker does not then *immediately* begin to take the hit, the Umpire will blow his whistle and act as in Penalty 7 (d).

(f) As soon as the ball is touched or hit in any way after the order "Play", this will be taken to be the free hit.

(g) You are reminded that delay is sometimes caused deliberately, not only for the sake of "teeing-up", but also to allow a pony to be changed, etc. For this reason, the practice of circling to get on the right leading leg, or any reason, is also to be disallowed, either at the beginning of the run-up or at the end of it.

In addition, Umpires attention was drawn to the rule that the interval between chukkas was 3 minutes. It was accepted that the 5 minute interval at half-time was not enforceable due to the practice of "treading in".

UMPIRES AND REFEREES HAND SIGNALS

In order to reduce the time taken in discussions between the Umpires and the Referee, the Chairman of the Umpires' Sub-Committee issued the following directive before season 1975:-

"Hand signals"

(a) The Umpires having consulted each other, turn towards the Referee and one of them raises his hand (this is to show that they disagree).

(b) If, in the Referee's opinion, no foul occurred, he will make the wash-out signal by a horizontal movement of both arms across his front.

(c) If he thinks a foul has occurred and it is obvious which side fouled, he will raise his hand above his head.

(d) If he is in any doubt whatsoever about any aspect of the affair, he will stand up but will make no signal at all, upon which the Umpires will canter up to consult him.

(e) The Umpires may wish to consult him in any case, in which case they will naturally canter straight up to him without making any signals.

(f) There is no reason why the Umpires should not ask the Referee which side fouled if they are in any doubt.

NEAR SIDE OFFENCES
Taking the ball on the near side

The relevant rules on the subject are Field Rule 16 (f) (Player to take the ball on off side) which reads as follows:-

"The Right of Way entitles a player to take the ball on the off side of his pony. If he places himself to hit it on the near side and thereby in any way endangers another player who would otherwise have been clear, he loses the Right of Way and must give way to this other player."
and Field Rule 17 (Dangerous Riding):-

(b) "Zigzagging in front of another player riding at a gallop in such a way as to cause the latter to check his pace or risk a fall."

(c) "Pulling across or over a pony's legs in such a manner as to risk tripping the pony etc."

There is nothing in the Rules to prevent a player taking the ball on the near side provided, as in any other manoeuvre, he does not endanger another player by doing so. It must be remembered that in high goal polo, the pace is faster than in low and medium, and the faster the horse is going, the longer it takes him to pull up. The safety distance in high goal polo is therefore greater than in low. It would appear that several accidents occurred in Argentina by players moving over to take the ball on the near side in order to avoid having their sticks hooked, and as the pace is so fast in much of their polo, umpires were obviously instructed to be less lenient in interpreting Rule 16 (f). They have complied with this to such an extent that many Argentine players appear to think that it is now against the rules to take the ball on the near side at all, and this idea has worked through into the umpiring in England and other places.

We think that this policy has now gone too far and that interpretation of Rule 16 (f) and 17 in this respect should be made slightly more lenient. This manoeuvre can, of course, be penalised under either Rule 16 (f) or 17 (b) and (c). Umpires are therefore directed that a player may move over and take the ball on the near side, provided there is sufficient distance between him and the other player not to endanger the latter; the important words being in 16 (f) ". . . . and thereby endangers another player". The other guiding principle is that the faster the polo, the greater the safety distance that must be allowed.

It is, of course, a foul to take the ball on the near side if an opponent is meeting it correctly, Rule 16 (g).

DAMAGED BALL

(a) Example. The ball splits into two parts and one part goes through the goal. If it is clear that the larger part of the ball goes through the goal the Umpires will normally award a goal. If the parts are about equal, the Umpires have to use their discretion and decide one way or the other. If a goal is not awarded, Field Rule 14 may be applied.

(b) Example. The ball splits or breaks up when struck in the course of a penalty being taken. Umpires, in this case, should allow the penalty to be taken again. But presumably they may decide the ball has not broken up sufficiently and that the larger part is still in play or has gone through or past the goal.
The following are further extracts from recent Umpires' meetings:-

THROW-INS

Although this problem is mentioned at every Meeting, Umpires are still failing to do as they are asked, namely:-

(a) "Throw-ins" from the Centre.
  (i) Keep the players behind the mark.
  (ii) Stop them charging the Umpire.
  (iii) Keep 10 yards back from the mark.
(b) "Throw-ins" from the Side
  (i) Place your horses hind legs on the side line.
  (ii) Keep the players a further 5 yards away from you.
  (iii) Keep them still.

POLO WORLDWIDE

The following list shows where polo is played today. The list is not exclusive and hopefully will grow as time progresses. For ease of reference I have split countries concerned into geographical regions.

EUROPE
Great Britain, France, Germany, Ireland, Italy, Spain and Switzerland.

NORTH AMERICA
Canada, Mexico and United States of America.

CENTRAL AMERICA
Costa Rica, Dominican Republic and Guatemala.

SOUTH AMERICA
Argentina, Brazil, Chile, Columbia, Equador, Paraguay, Peru, Uruguay and Venezuela.

AFRICA
Burundi, Egypt, Ethiopia, Ghana, Kenya, Nigeria, South Africa, Sudan, Zambia and Zimbabwe.

MIDDLE EAST
Cyprus, Dubai, Jordan, Malta and Oman.

FAR EAST
Australia, Brunei, Hong Kong, India, Malaysia, New Zealand, Pakistan, Phillipines and Singapore.

CONCLUSION

There has been a significant rise in the standard of polo in recent years; there are many reasons for this, including the existence of polo schools and polo scholarships. However, except in Argentina, there is a scarcity of middle-handicapped players. It seems that many "1 goal" players think that there is little more for them to learn.

In all other sports the better the standard the more the participants are coached. When an event is televised the camera frequently focuses on the coach, presumably because the audience will have more respect for the sport once they know that he, or she, exists. Surely polo should align itself with other games and not allow misguided tradition to suggest the attitude "I will not be the first to have a coach on the sideline". For this to happen Polo Associations must encourage and coordinate a system of instruction which embraces tactics, riding and striking in a similar manner to that described in this book.

I suspect that some readers are thinking "If I was coached, how could I have the opportunity to participate sufficiently for all these points to be watched?" This highlights the necessity for a new attitude which would provide more involvement for all players. A simple way to achieve this would be to request the best player in each team, preferably the No.3, during club chukkas not to attempt to score goals. Thus he would have to distribute the ball constructively instead of looking for the goal, thereby giving extra valuable experience to players with less ability.

The few professionals who ridicule team mates as "slow idiots" or opponents as "dangerous louts" should be made to realise that the unique mixing of such different standards in polo must be tolerated with patience in order that the sport can be financed and allow them to travel to play in exotic places. Confidence and courage will only be accrued by those with low handicaps if they are allowed more of the ball so that they can adjust to their mistakes.

All players should understand that it is easier for a coach to influence others when he has no direct involvement with them on the field of play. No one can possibly think that a sideline coach should himself score goals instead of telling others what to do. In fact he can relieve the best player of considerable pressure by suggesting tactics which will blend the different standards effectively together.